Birds of Colorado

Field Guide

by Stan Tekiela

ADVENTURE PUBLICATIONS, INC.
CAMBRIDGE, MINNESOTA

TO MY WIFE KATHERINE AND DAUGHTER ABIGAIL
WITH ALL MY LOVE

ACKNOWLEDGMENTS:

Special thanks to Anthony Hertzel for range maps, and Tony Leukering, Monitoring Coordinator, Rocky Mountain Bird Observatory, and author, illustrator and photographer Brian K. Wheeler for reviewing them. Special thanks also to Sandy Livoti for her exceptional eye to detail.

Book design and illustrations by Jonathan Norberg

Photo credits by photographer and page number:

Cover photo: Lazuli Bunting by Brian E. Small
Dominique Braud: 284 (adult) **Brian Collins**: 170 **Cornell Laboratory of Ornithology**: 72, 74 (female), 212 (both) **Dembinsky Photo Associates**: 30, 242 (both), 256 (both) **Dudley Edmondson**: 12, 14, 20, 22, 24, 26 (soaring), 52 (soaring), 54 (all), 76, 80, 84, 88 (female), 96, 100 (both), 120, 122, 134 (in flight), 138, 144 (both), 146 (yellow-shafted male), 150, 162 (soaring light morph), 164 (both), 168, 192 (male), 202, 208, 210 (male), 218 (both), 220, 222, 224 (breeding), 232, 276 (breeding), 288 (male, winter male), 290, 294 (male), 306 **Don Enger**: 50 (rushing, weed dance) **Kevin T. Karlson**: 42 (breeding), 160, 278 (breeding), 280 **Bill Marchel**: 4, 6, 32 (male), 40, 74 (male), 78, 112 (white-striped), 140, 156, 172 (female), 190, 192 (female), 238, 250, 252, 274 **Maslowski Wildlife Productions**: 8 (male), 36 (male), 60, 62, 66 (female), 94, 102 (male), 104 (male), 110, 128, 178, 180, 186, 240 (male), 244 (male), 268, 284 (chick-feeding adult), 296, 302, 308 **Steve Mortensen**: 10, 32 (female), 38 (both), 44, 52 (perching), 58, 68, 98 (both), 154, 182, 288 (female), 304 (both) **Warren Nelson**: 16, 146 (yellow-shafted female), 294 (female) **John Pennoyer**: 46, 82, 130, 254, 264 (male) **Brian E. Small**: 2, 8, 8 (female), 28 (breeding and non-breeding males), 34 (both), 36 (female), 42 (winter), 50 (breeding), 64 (both), 66 (male), 70, 88 (Oregon female, gray-headed), 90, 92, 102 (female), 104 (female), 106, 108 (female), 116, 124, 126 (winter), 146 (red-shafted male and female), 152, 158, 174 (perching), 188 (Oregon male), 194, 196, 198, 200, 204, 206, 216, 224 (winter), 230, 240 (female), 244 (female), 246, 248, 258, 260, 262, 264 (yellow male), 266, 276 (winter, juvenile), 278 (winter), 286 (female), 292, 298 (all), 300 **Stan Tekiela**: 18, 48, 56, 86, 112 (tan-striped), 114 (both), 118, 126 (breeding), 132, 134 (perching), 136, 142, 148, 166, 172 (male), 176, 184, 188 (male), 210 (female), 214, 228, 234, 236, 270, 272, 282 (all), 286 (male) **Brian K. Wheeler**: 26 (perching), 162 (perching light and dark morphs, soaring dark morph, intermediate morph), 174 (soaring, juvenile), 226 (both)

To the best of the publisher's knowledge, all photos were of live birds.

Fourth Printing
Copyright 2001 by Stan Tekiela
Published by Adventure Publications, Inc.
820 Cleveland Street South
Cambridge, MN 55008
1-800-678-7006

TABLE OF CONTENTS

Introduction

Sample Page

The Birds

WHY WATCH BIRDS IN COLORADO?

Millions of people have discovered bird feeding. It's a simple and enjoyable way to bring the beauty of birds closer to your home. Watching birds at your feeder often leads to a lifetime pursuit of bird identification. The *Birds of Colorado Field Guide* is for those who want to identify common birds of Colorado.

There are over 800 species of birds found in North America. In Colorado alone there have been more than 460 different kinds of birds recorded through the years. These bird sightings were diligently recorded by hundreds of bird watchers and became part of the official state record. From these valuable records, I've chosen 130 of the most common birds of Colorado to include in this field guide.

Bird watching, often called birding, is the largest spectator sport in America. Its outstanding popularity in Colorado is due, in part, to an unusually rich and abundant birdlife. Why are there so many birds? One reason is open space. Colorado is more than 104,000 square miles (270,400 sq. km), making it the eighth largest state. Despite its size, only about 4 million people call Colorado home. On average, that's only 39 people per square mile (15 per sq. km). Most of these people are located in and around only four major cities, all of which line up in a narrow belt of about 200 miles (322 km) along the eastern foothills of the Rockies. Over 80 percent of the state's population lives in an urban environment. This concentration of people leaves plenty of room for birds.

Open space is not the only reason there is such an abundance of birds. It's also the diversity of habitat. The state can be broken into three distinct habitats—plains, mountains and plateaus—each of which supports a different group of birds.

The eastern one-third of the state is composed of a flat or gently rolling terrain known as the Great Plains. This region is home to many open country birds such as the Lark Bunting, which is also the official state bird of Colorado.

Dividing the state down the middle is the southern extension of the Rocky Mountains. These mountains, with more than 50 peaks–many over 14,000 feet (4,250 m)–are a great place to see alpine birds and more. Birds such as the Mountain Chickadee and Cassin's Finch call this mountainous region home.

To the west of the Rockies lies the Colorado Plateau. This region stands between 5,000 and 11,000 feet (1,500 to 3,350 m). Its many hills and valleys are home to such birds as the Common Raven and Green-tailed Towhee.

Water also plays a part in Colorado's bird populations. There are over 371 sq. miles (965 sq. km) of water surface in the state. From the Colorado River to the Arkansas River, this essential element supports a wide variety of water-loving birds such as the American White Pelican and American Avocet.

Varying habitats in Colorado also mean variations in weather. Since elevation in the state rises from approximately 4,000 feet (1,200 m) in the eastern plains to over 14,000 feet (4,250 m) at mountaintops, there are great differences in weather. Tall peaks, such as Pikes Peak, Mount Evans and Blanca Peak, are some of the coldest and snowiest places in Colorado, while the Great Plains region is the beneficiary of warming air as it moves down from the high country.

In hot weather or cold, in elevations low or high and anywhere in between, there are birds in Colorado to watch in each season. Whether witnessing a migration of hawks in fall or welcoming back hummingbirds in spring, there is variety and excitement in birding as each season turns to the next.

OBSERVE WITH A STRATEGY; TIPS FOR IDENTIFYING BIRDS

Identifying birds isn't as difficult as you might think. By simply following a few basic strategies, you can increase your chances of successfully identifying most birds you see! One of the first and easiest things to do when you see a new bird is to note its color. (Also, since this book is organized by color, you will go right to that color section to find it.)

Next, note the size of the bird. A strategy to quickly estimate size is to select a small-, medium- and large-sized bird to use for reference. For example, most people are familiar with robins. A robin, measured from tip of the bill to tip of the tail, is 10 inches (25 cm) long. Using the robin as an example of a medium-sized bird, select two other birds, one smaller and one larger. Many people use a House Sparrow, at about 6 inches (15 cm), and an American Crow, about 18 inches (45 cm). When you see a bird that you don't know, you can quickly ask yourself, "Is it smaller than a robin, but larger than a sparrow?" When you look in your field guide to help identify your bird, you'll know it's roughly between 6 and 10 inches (15 to 25 cm) long. This will help to narrow your choices.

Next, note the size, shape and color of the bill. Is it long, short, thick, thin, pointed, blunt, curved or straight? Seed-eating birds, such as Evening Grosbeaks, have bills that are thick and strong enough to crack even the toughest seeds. Birds that sip nectar, such as Black-chinned Hummingbirds, need long thin bills to reach deep into flowers. Hawks and owls tear their prey with very sharp, curving bills. Sometimes, just noting the bill shape can help you decide if the bird is a woodpecker, finch, grosbeak, blackbird or bird of prey.

Next, take a look around and note the habitat in which you see the bird. Is it wading in a marsh? Walking along a riverbank? Soaring in the sky? Is it perched high in the trees or hopping along the forest floor? Because of their preferences in diet and habitat, you'll usually see robins hopping on the ground, but not often eating the seeds at your feeder. Or you'll see a Blue Grosbeak sitting on a branch of a tree, but not climbing down the tree trunk headfirst the way a nuthatch does.

Noticing what a bird is eating will give you another clue to help you identify that bird. Feeding is a big part of any bird's life. Fully one-third of all bird activity revolves around searching for and catching food, or actually eating. While birds don't always follow all the rules of what we think they eat, you can make some general assumptions. Northern Flickers, for instance, feed upon ants and other insects, so you wouldn't expect to see them visiting a backyard bird feeder. Some birds, such as the Barn Swallow and the Tree Swallow, feed on flying insects, and spend hours swooping and diving to catch a meal.

Sometimes you can identify a bird by the way it perches. Body posture can help you differentiate between an American Crow and a Red-tailed Hawk. American Crows lean forward over their feet on a branch, while hawks perch in a vertical position. Look for this the next time you see a large unidentified bird in a tree.

Birds in flight are often difficult to identify, but noting the size and shape of the wing will help. A bird's wing size is in direct proportion to its body size, weight and type of flying. The shape of the wing determines if the bird flies fast and with precision, or slowly and less precisely. Birds such as House Finches, which flit around thick tangles of branches, have short round wings. Birds that soar on warm updrafts of air, such as Turkey Vultures, have long broad wings. Barn Swallows have short pointed wings that slice through air, propelling their swift and accurate flight.

Some birds have unique flight patterns that aid in identification. American Goldfinches fly in a distinctive up-and-down pattern that makes it look as if they are riding a roller coaster.

While it's not easy to make these observations in the short time you often have to watch a "mystery bird," practicing these methods of identification will greatly expand your skills in birding. Also, seek the guidance of a more experienced birder who will help you improve your skills and answer questions on the spot.

BIRD BASICS

It's easier to identify birds and communicate about them if you know the names of the different parts of a bird. For instance, it's much easier to use the word "crest" to indicate the erect feathers on the head of a Steller's Jay than trying to describe them.

The following illustration points out the basic parts of a bird. Because it is a composite of many birds, it shouldn't be confused with any actual bird.

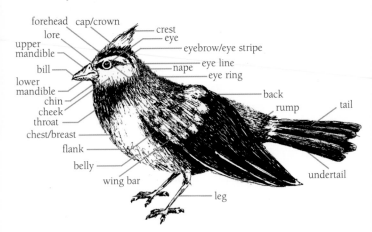

BIRD COLOR VARIABLES

No other animal has a color pallet like a bird's. Brilliant blues, lemon yellows, showy reds and iridescent greens are common-place within the bird world. In general, the male birds are more colorful than their female counterparts. This is probably to help the male attract a mate, essentially saying, "Hey, look at me!" It also calls attention to the male's overall health. The better the condition of his feathers, the better his food source and territory, and therefore, the better his potential for a mate.

Female birds that don't look like their male counterparts (such species are called sexually dimorphic, meaning "two forms") are often a nondescript color, as seen with the Blue Grosbeak. These muted tones help hide the females during weeks of motionless incubation, and draw less attention to them when they are out feeding or taking a break from the rigors of raising young.

In some species, such as the Bald Eagle, Blue Jay and Downy Woodpecker, the male birds look nearly identical to the females. In the case of the woodpeckers, the sexes are only differentiated by a single red or sometimes yellow mark. Depending on the species, the mark may be on top of the head, face, nape of the neck or just behind the bill.

During the first year, juvenile birds often look like the mothers. Since brightly colored feathers are used mainly for attracting a mate, young non-breeding males don't have a need for colorful plumage. It is not until the first spring molt (or several years later, depending on the species) that young males obtain their breeding colors.

Both breeding and winter plumages are the result of molting. Molting is the process of dropping old worn feathers and replacing them with new ones. All birds molt, typically twice a year, with the spring molt usually occurring in late winter. During this time, most birds produce their breeding plumage (brighter colors for attracting mates), which lasts throughout the summer.

Winter plumage is the result of the late summer molt, which serves a couple of important functions. First, it adds feathers for warmth in the coming winter. Second, in some species it produces feathers that tend to be drab in color, which helps to camouflage the birds and hide them from predators. The winter plumage of the male American Goldfinch, for example, is an olive brown, unlike its obvious canary yellow color in summer. Luckily for us, some birds, such as Lewis's Woodpeckers, retain their bright summer colors all year long.

BIRD NESTS

Bird nests are truly an amazing feat of engineering. Imagine building your home strong enough to weather a storm, large enough to hold your entire family, insulated enough to shelter them from cold and heat, and waterproof enough to keep out rain. Now, build it without any blueprints or directions, and without the use of your hands or feet! Birds do!

Before building a nest, an appropriate site must be selected. With some birds, such as the House Wren, the male picks out several potential sites and assembles several small twigs in each. This discourages other birds from using nearby nest cavities. These "extra" nests are occasionally called dummy nests. The female is then taken around and shown all the choices. She chooses her favorite and finishes constructing the nest. With some other species of birds, for example, the Bullock's Oriole, it's the female who chooses the site and builds the nest with the male only offering an occasional suggestion. Each bird species has its own nest-building routine, which is strictly followed.

Nesting material usually consists of natural elements found in the immediate area. Most nests consist of plant fibers (such as bark peeled from grapevines), sticks, mud, dried grass, feathers, fur, or soft fuzzy tufts from thistle. Some birds, including the Black-chinned Hummingbird, use spider webs to glue nest materials together. Nesting material is limited to what a bird can hold or carry. Because of this, a bird must make many trips afield to gather enough materials to complete its nest. Most nests take at least four days or more, and hundreds, if not thousands, of trips to build.

As you'll see in the following illustrations, birds build a wide variety of nest types.

ground nest   platform nest   cup nest   pendulous nest

The simple **ground nest** is scraped out of earth. These shallow depressions usually contain no nesting material, and are made by birds such as the Killdeer and Horned Lark.

Another kind of nest, the **platform nest**, represents a more complex type of nest building. Constructed of small twigs and branches, the platform nest is a simple arrangement of sticks which forms a platform and features a small depression to nestle the eggs.

Some platform nests, such as those of the Canada Goose, are constructed on the ground, and are made of mud and grass. Platform nests can also be on cliffs, bridges, balconies or even in flowerpots. This kind of nest gives space to adventurous youngsters, and functions as a landing platform for the parents. Many waterfowl construct platform nests on the ground, usually near water or actually in the water. These floating platform nests vary with the water level, thus preventing nests with eggs from being flooded. Platform nests, constructed by such birds as Mourning Doves and herons, are not anchored to the tree, and may tumble from the branches during high winds and storms.

The **cup nest** is a modified platform nest, used by three-quarters of all songbirds. Constructed from the outside in, a supporting platform is constructed first. This platform is attached firmly to a tree, shrub or rock ledge. Next, the sides are constructed of grasses, small twigs, bark or leaves, which are woven together and often glued with mud for additional strength. The inner cup, lined with feathers, animal fur, soft plant material or animal hair, is constructed last. The mother bird uses her chest to cast the final contours of the inner nest.

The **pendulous nest** is an unusual nest, looking more like a sock hanging from a branch than a nest. Inaccessible to most predators, these nests are attached to the ends of the smallest branches of a tree, and often wave wildly in the breeze. Woven very tightly of plant fibers, they are strong and watertight, taking up to a week to build. More commonly used by tropical birds, this complicated nest type has also been mastered by orioles and kinglets. A small opening on the top or side allows the parents access to the grass-lined interior. (It must be one heck of a ride to be inside one of these nests during a windy spring thunderstorm!)

One of the most clever of all nest types is known as the **no nest** or daycare nest. Parasitic birds, such as Brown-headed Cowbirds, build no nests at all! The egg-laden female expertly searches out other birds' nests and sneaks in to lay one of her own eggs while the host mother is not looking, thereby leaving the host mother to raise an adopted youngster. The mother cowbird wastes no energy building a nest only to have it raided by a predator. By using several nests of other birds, she spreads out her progeny in hope that at least one of her offspring will live to maturity.

Another type of nest, the **cavity nest**, is used by many birds, including woodpeckers and Western Bluebirds. The cavity nest is usually excavated in a tree branch or trunk, and offers shelter from storms, sun, predators and cold. A relatively small entrance hole in a tree leads to an inner chamber up to 10 inches (25 cm) below. Usually constructed by woodpeckers, the cavity nest is typically used only once by its builder, but subsequently can be used for many years by birds such as mergansers, Tree Swallows and bluebirds, which do not have the capability of excavating one for themselves. Kingfishers, on the other hand, excavate a tunnel up to 4 feet (1 m) long, which connects the entrance in a riverbank to the nest chamber. These cavity nests are often sparsely lined because they are already well insulated.

Some birds, including some swallows, take nest building one step further. They use a collection of small balls of mud to construct an adobe-style home. Constructed under the eaves of houses, under bridges or inside chimneys, some of these nests look like simple cup nests. Others are completely enclosed, with small tunnel-like openings that lead into a safe nesting chamber for the baby birds.

WHO BUILDS THE NEST?

In general, the female bird builds the nest. She gathers nesting materials and constructs a nest, with an occasional visit from her mate to check on the progress. In some species, both parents contribute equally to the construction of a nest. A male bird might forage for precisely the right sticks, grass or mud, but it's often the female that forms or puts together the nest. She uses her body to form the egg chamber. Rarely does the male build a nest by himself.

FLEDGING

Fledging is the interval between hatching and flight or leaving the nest. Some birds leave the nest within hours of hatching (precocial), but it might be weeks before they are able to fly. This is common with waterfowl and shorebirds. Until they start to fly, they are called fledglings. Birds that are still in the nest are called nestlings. Other baby birds are born naked and blind, and remain in the nest for several weeks (altricial).

WHY BIRDS MIGRATE

Why do birds migrate? The short answer is simple–food. Birds migrate to areas of high food concentrations. It is easier to breed where food is than where it is not. A typical migrating bird, the Western Tanager, for instance, will migrate from the tropics of Central America and Mexico to nest in forests of North America, taking advantage of the billions of newly hatched insects to feed its young. This trip is called **complete migration**.

Some birds of prey return from their complete migration to northern regions that are overflowing with small rodents, such as mice and voles, that have continued to breed in winter.

Complete migrators have a set time and pattern of migration. Each year at nearly the same time, they take off and head for a specific wintering ground. Complete migrators may travel great distances, sometimes as much as 15,000 miles (24,150 km) or more in a year. But complete migration doesn't necessarily imply flying from the cold, frozen northland to a tropical destination. The Dark-eyed Junco, for example, is a complete migrator that flies from the far reaches of Canada to spend the winter right here in Colorado.

There are many interesting aspects to complete migrators. In the spring, males usually migrate several weeks before the females, arriving early to scope out possibilities for nesting sites and food sources, and to begin to defend territories. The females arrive several weeks later. In the autumn, in many species, the females and their young leave early, often up to four weeks before the adult males.

Not all migrators are the same. There are **partial migrators**, such as American Goldfinches, that usually wait until food supplies dwindle before they fly south. Unlike complete migrators, the partial migrators move only far enough south, or sometimes east and west, to find abundant food. Some years it might be only a few hundred miles, while other years it might be nearly a thousand. This kind of migration, dependent upon the weather and available food, is sometimes called **seasonal movement**.

Unlike the predictable ebbing and flowing behavior of complete migrators or partial migrators, **irruptive migrators** can move every third to fifth year, or in some cases, in consecutive years. These migrations are triggered when times are really tough and food is scarce. Red-breasted Nuthatches are a good example of irruptive migrators, because they leave their normal northern range in search of food or in response to overpopulation.

HOW DO BIRDS MIGRATE?

One of the many secrets of migration is fat. While we humans are fighting the battle of the bulge, birds intentionally gorge themselves to put on as much fat as possible while still being able to fly. Fat provides the greatest amount of energy per unit of weight, and in the same way that your car needs gas, birds are propelled by fat or stalled without it.

During long migratory flights, fat deposits are used up quickly, and birds need to stop to "refuel." This is when backyard bird feeding stations and undeveloped, natural spaces around our towns and cities are especially important. Some birds require up to two to three days of constant feeding to build up their fat reserves before continuing their seasonal trip.

Some birds, such as most eagles, hawks, ospreys, falcons and vultures, migrate during the day. Larger birds can hold more body fat, go longer without eating and take longer to migrate. These birds glide along on rising columns of warm air, called thermals, which hold them aloft while they slowly make their way north or south. They generally rest at night and hunt early in the morning before the sun has a chance to warm up the land and create good soaring conditions. Birds migrating during the day use a combination of landforms, rivers, and the rising and setting sun to guide them in the right direction.

Most other birds migrate during the night. Studies show that some birds which migrate at night use the stars to navigate. Others use the setting sun, while still others, such as doves, use the earth's magnetic fields to guide them north or south. While flying at night might seem like a crazy idea, nocturnal migration is safer for several reasons. First, there are fewer nighttime predators for migrating birds. Second, traveling at night allows time during the day to find food in unfamiliar surroundings. Finally, nighttime wind patterns tend to be flat, or laminar. These flat winds don't have the turbulence associated with the daytime winds, and can actually help carry smaller birds by pushing them along.

HOW TO USE THIS GUIDE

To help you quickly and easily identify birds, this book is organized by color. Simply note the color of the bird and turn to that section. Refer to the first page for the color key. The Red-headed Woodpecker, for example, is black and white with a red head. Because the bird is mostly black and white, it will be found in the black and white section. Each color section is also arranged by size, generally with the smaller birds first. Sections may also incorporate the average size in a range, which in some cases reflects size differences between the male and female birds. Flip through the pages in that color section to find the bird. If you already know the name of the bird, check the index for the page number. In some species, the male and female are remarkably different in color. In these cases, the opposite sex is shown in a smaller inset photograph with a page reference. These birds, therefore, will be found in two different color sections.

In the description section you will find a variety of information about the bird. On the next page is a sample of the information included in the book.

RANGE MAPS

Range maps are included for each bird. Colored areas indicate where in Colorado a particular bird is most likely to be found. Green is used for summer, blue for winter, red for year-round and yellow for areas where the bird is seen during migration. While every effort has been made to accurately depict these ranges, they are only general guidelines. Ranges actually change on an ongoing basis due to a variety of factors. Changes in weather, species abundance, landscape and vital resources such as the availability of food and water can affect local populations, migration and movements, causing birds to be found in areas not typical for the species.

Colored areas simply mean bird sightings for that species have been frequent in those areas and less frequent in the others. Please use the maps as intended–as general guides only.

COMMON NAME
Scientific name

COLOR INDICATOR

YEAR-ROUND
MIGRATION
SUMMER
WINTER

Size: measures head to tail, may include wingspan

Male: a brief description of the male bird, and may include breeding, winter or other plumages

Female: a brief description of the female bird, which is sometimes not the same as the male

Juvenile: a brief description of the juvenile bird, which often looks like the female

Nest: the kind of nest this bird builds to raise its young, who builds the nest, and how many broods per year

Eggs: how many eggs you might expect to see in a nest, and the color of the eggs

Incubation: the average time the parents spend incubating the eggs, and who does the incubation

Fledging: the average time the young spend in the nest after hatching but before they leave the nest, and which parent(s) does most of the "child-care" and feeding

Migration: type of migration: complete (consistent, seasonal), or partial (seasonal, destination varies), or irruptive (unpredictable, depending on the food supply), or non-migrator

Food: what the bird eats most of the time (e.g., seeds, nectar, insects, fruit, small animals), and if it typically comes to a bird feeding station

Compare: notes about other birds that look similar, and the pages on which they can be found

Stan's Notes: Interesting gee-whiz natural history information. This could be something to look or listen for, or something to help positively identify the bird. Also includes remarkable features.

BLACK ROSY-FINCH
Leucosticte atrata

WINTER

Size: 6" (15 cm)

Male: Dark gray to nearly black overall. Light gray band around back of head from eye to eye. Areas of rosy red on wings and belly. Small dark bill with a small white mark near base of upper bill.

Female: same as male, but has less pink

Juvenile: similar to adults, but a light gray, lacks rosy red color and has a yellow bill

Nest: cup; female builds; 1-2 broods per year

Eggs: 3-5; white without markings

Incubation: 12-14 days; female incubates

Fledging: 16-18 days; female and male feed young

Migration: partial migrator, moves around in higher elevations to find food

Food: seeds, insects, will visit seed feeders

Compare: Similar to the other rosy-finches (pp. 103 and 105), but tends to be the darkest with the least amount of rosy red on body and only a small amount of gray on head.

Stan's Notes: A winter resident found in the high alpine regions, nesting in faces of steep cliffs. One of the few species in which the female determines territory and chooses a nest site. Consequently, the male has a poorly developed song because it doesn't need it to attract mates or defend territories. During breeding, both male and female develop an opening in the floor of mouth (buccal pouch), which is used to carry a large supply of food, such as insects, to the young in the nest. Doesn't breed in Colorado.

3

female pg. 123

male

BROWN-HEADED COWBIRD
Molothrus ater

SUMMER

Size: 7½" (19 cm)

Male: A glossy black bird, reminiscent of a Red-winged Blackbird. Chocolate brown head with a pointed, sharp gray bill.

Female: dull brown bird with bill similar to male

Juvenile: similar to female, only dull gray color and a streaked chest

Nest: no nest; lays eggs in nests of other birds

Eggs: 5-7; white with brown markings

Incubation: 10-13 days; host bird incubates eggs

Fledging: 10-11 days; host birds feed young

Migration: complete, to southern states

Food: insects, seeds, will come to seed feeders

Compare: The male Red-winged Blackbird (pg. 11) is slightly larger, with red and yellow patches on upper wings. Common Grackle (pg. 17) has a long tail and lacks the brown head. European Starling (pg. 7) has a shorter tail.

Stan's Notes: A member of the blackbird family. Of approximately 750 species of parasitic birds worldwide, this is the only parasitic bird in Colorado, laying all eggs in host birds' nests, leaving others to raise its young. Cowbirds are known to have laid eggs in nests of over 200 species of birds. Some birds reject cowbird eggs, but most raise them, even to the exclusion of their own young. Look for warblers and other birds feeding young birds twice their own size. At one time cowbirds followed bison to feed on the insects attracted to the animals.

EUROPEAN STARLING
Sturnus vulgaris

Size: 7½" (19 cm)

Male: Iridescent purple black bird covered with white speckles during autumn and winter. Shiny purple black in spring and summer. Long, pointed yellow bill in the spring and gray in autumn. Short tail.

Female: same as male

Juvenile: similar to adult, only a gray brown with a streaked chest

Nest: cavity; male and female line the cavity; 2 broods per year

Eggs: 4-6; bluish with brown markings

Incubation: 12-14 days; female and male incubate

Fledging: 18-20 days; female and male feed young

Migration: non-migrator to partial migrator, some will move to southern states

Food: insects, seeds, fruit, comes to seed and suet feeders

Compare: Looks similar to Common Grackle (pg. 17), but lacks its long tail.

Stan's Notes: A great songster, it is also able to mimic sounds. Often displaces woodpeckers, chickadees and other cavity-nesting birds. Can be very aggressive and destroy eggs or young of other birds. The bill changes color with the seasons: yellow in spring and gray in autumn. Jaws are designed to be the most powerful when opening, as they pry open crevices to locate hidden insects. Gathers in the hundreds in autumn. Not a native bird, it was introduced to New York City in 1890-91 from Europe.

male

female

SPOTTED TOWHEE
Pipilo maculatus

YEAR-ROUND
MIGRATION
SUMMER
WINTER

Size: 8½" (22 cm)

Male: A mostly black bird with dirty-red-brown sides and white belly. Multiple white spots on wings and sides. Long black tail with a white tip. Rich red eyes.

Female: same as male, but a brown head

Juvenile: brown with heavily streaked chest

Nest: cup; female builds; 1-2 broods per year

Eggs: 3-5; white with brown markings

Incubation: 12-14 days; female and male incubate

Fledging: 10-12 days; female and male feed young

Migration: partial migrator, to Texas and Mexico

Food: seeds, fruit, insects

Compare: Closely related to the Green-tailed Towhee (pg. 247), which appears nothing like the bold black and red of the Spotted Towhee.

Stan's Notes: Not as common as the Green-tailed Towhee, but it inhabits a similar habitat. Most found between 5,000- and 7,000-foot (1,500 to 2,150 m) elevations in oak scrub country. Often heard noisily scratching around through dead leaves on the ground, searching for food. Over 70 percent of the diet is plant material, consuming more insects in spring and summer. Well known for retreating from danger by walking away rather than taking to flight. Female builds nest, nearly always on the ground beneath bushes, but away from where the male perches to sing. Song and plumage vary geographically and are not well studied or understood.

female pg. 131

male

RED-WINGED BLACKBIRD
Agelaius phoeniceus

YEAR-ROUND
SUMMER

Size: 8½" (22 cm)

Male: Jet black bird with red and yellow shoulder patches on upper wings. Pointed black bill.

Female: heavily streaked brown bird with a pointed brown bill and white eyebrows

Juvenile: same as female

Nest: cup; female builds; 2-3 broods per year

Eggs: 3-4; bluish green with brown markings

Incubation: 10-12 days; female incubates

Fledging: 11-14 days; female and male feed young

Migration: partial migrator to non-migrator, will move around the state to find food in winter

Food: seeds, insects, will come to seed feeders

Compare: Slightly larger than the male Brown-headed Cowbird (pg. 5), but is less iridescent and lacks Cowbird's brown head. Differs from all blackbirds due to the red and yellow patches on its wings (epaulets).

Stan's Notes: One of the most widespread and numerous birds in Colorado. It is a sure sign of spring when Red-winged Blackbirds return to the marshes. Flocks of up to 100,000 birds have been reported. Males return before the females and defend territories by singing from the tops of surrounding vegetation. Will repeat call from top of cattail while showing off its red and yellow wing bars (epaulets). Nests are usually over shallow water in thick stands of cattails. They feed mostly on seeds in spring and fall, switching to insects during summer. Females choose mate.

11

female pg. 133

male

BREWER'S BLACKBIRD
Euphagus cyanocephalus

YEAR-ROUND
SUMMER

Size: 9" (22.5 cm)

Male: Overall glossy black, shining green in direct light. Head more purple than green. Bright white or pale yellow eyes. Winter plumage can be dull gray to black.

Female: similar to male, only overall grayish brown, most have dark eyes

Juvenile: similar to female

Nest: cup; female builds; 1-2 broods per year

Eggs: 4-6; gray with brown markings

Incubation: 12-14 days; female incubates

Fledging: 13-14 days; female and male feed young

Migration: complete, southwestern states and Mexico, partial to non-migrator in parts of Colorado

Food: insects, seeds, fruit

Compare: Smaller than the Common Grackle (pg. 17) and the male Great-tailed Grackle (pg. 21), lacking the long tail of both species. Male Brown-headed Cowbird (pg. 5) is smaller and has a brown head.

Stan's Notes: A common blackbird of open areas such as farms, wet pastures, mountain meadows up to 10,000 feet (3,050 m) and even desert scrub. Usually nests in a shrub, small tree or directly on the ground. Prefers nesting in small colonies of up to 20 pairs. Doesn't get along with Common Grackles, often being driven out of nesting areas by expansion of the grackles. Will flock with other species such as Red-winged Blackbirds and cowbirds. A common cowbird host.

female pg. 139

male

YELLOW-HEADED BLACKBIRD
Xanthocephalus xanthocephalus

SUMMER

Size: 9-11" (22.5-28 cm)

Male: Large black bird with a lemon-yellow head, chest and nape of neck. Black mask and a gray bill. White wing patches.

Female: similar to male, only slightly smaller with a brown body, dull yellow head and chest

Juvenile: similar to female

Nest: cup; female builds; 2 broods per year

Eggs: 3-5; greenish white with brown markings

Incubation: 11-13 days; female incubates

Fledging: 9-12 days; female feeds young

Migration: complete, to southern states and Mexico

Food: insects, seeds

Compare: Larger than the male Red-winged Blackbird (pg. 11), which has red and yellow patches on its wings. Male Yellow-headed Blackbird is the only large black bird with a bright yellow head.

Stan's Notes: Usually heard before seen, Yellow-headed Blackbird has a low, hoarse, raspy or metallic call. Nests in deep water marshes unlike its cousin, the Red-winged Blackbird, which prefers shallow water. The male gives an impressive mating display, flying with head drooped and feet and tail pointing down while steadily beating its wings. The female incubates alone and feeds between three to five young. Young keep low and out of sight for up to three weeks before they start to fly. Migrates in flocks of up to 200 with grackles and cowbirds. Flocks consisting mainly of males return in late March and early April. Most colonies consist of between 20 to 100 nests.

COMMON GRACKLE
Quiscalus quiscula

YEAR-ROUND
SUMMER

Size: 11-13" (28-33 cm)

Male: Large black bird with iridescent blue black head, purple brown body, long black tail, long thin bill and bright golden eyes.

Female: similar to male, only duller and smaller

Juvenile: similar to female

Nest: cup; female builds; 2 broods per year

Eggs: 4-5; greenish white with brown markings

Incubation: 13-14 days; female incubates

Fledging: 16-20 days; female and male feed young

Migration: complete to partial, to southern states

Food: fruit, seeds, insects, comes to seed feeders

Compare: Male Great-tailed Grackle (pg. 21) is larger and has a much longer tail. The European Starling (pg. 7) is much smaller, and has a speckled appearance and yellow bill. Male Brewer's Blackbird (pg. 13) is smaller and lacks the Common Grackle's long tail. Male Red-winged Blackbird (pg. 11) has red and yellow wing markings.

Stan's Notes: Usually nests in small colonies of up to 75 pairs, but travels with other blackbirds in large flocks. Is known to feed in farmers' fields. Name comes from the Latin word *graculus*, meaning "to cough," for its loud raspy call. Holds its tail in a keel-like position during flight. The flight pattern is almost always level, as opposed to having undulating up-and-down movements. Unlike most birds, has larger muscles to open mouth rather than to close it, as it pries open crevices to locate hidden insects.

17

AMERICAN COOT
Fulica americana

YEAR-ROUND
MIGRATION
SUMMER

Size: 13-16" (33-40 cm)

Male: Slate gray to black all over, white bill with dark band near tip. Green legs and feet. A small white patch near the base of the tail. Prominent red eyes, with a small red patch above bill between eyes.

Female: same as male

Juvenile: much paler than adult, with a gray bill and same white rump patch

Nest: floating platform; female and male build; 1 brood per year

Eggs: 9-12; pinkish buff with brown markings

Incubation: 21-25 days; female and male incubate

Fledging: 49-52 days; female and male feed young

Migration: complete, to southern states, Mexico and Central America

Food: insects, aquatic plants

Compare: Smaller than most waterfowl, it is the only black water bird or duck-like bird with a white bill.

Stan's Notes: An excellent diver and swimmer, often seen in large flocks on open water. Not a duck, as it doesn't have webbed feet, but instead has large lobed toes. When taking off, scrambles across the surface of the water with wings flapping. Bobs its head while swimming. Nest is a floating mat of vegetation. Huge flocks of up to 1,000 birds gather for fall migration. The unusual name is of unknown origin, but in Middle English, *coote* was used to describe various waterfowl–perhaps it stuck. Also called Mud-hen.

female pg. 151

male

GREAT-TAILED GRACKLE
Quiscalus mexicanus

SUMMER

Size: 18" (45 cm), male
15" (38 cm), female

Male: A large all-black bird with iridescent purple sheen on the head and back. Exceptionally long tail. Bright yellow eyes.

Female: considerably smaller than the male, overall brown bird with gray-to-brown belly, light brown eyes, eyebrows, throat, upper chest

Juvenile: similar to female

Nest: cup; female builds; 1-2 broods per year

Eggs: 3-5; greenish blue with brown markings

Incubation: 12-14 days; female incubates

Fledging: 21-23 days; female feeds young

Migration: partial migrator to complete, moves around to find food

Food: insects, fruit, seeds, comes to seed feeders

Compare: Common Grackle (pg. 17) is smaller, with a much shorter tail.

Stan's Notes: A bird that has expanded its range into Colorado recently, preferring to nest near water in an open habitat. Mainly in southern Colorado in elevations up to 8,000 feet (2,450 m), they are expanding northward and are expected to populate the entire state. Only a small percentage remains all winter. The rest move only far enough south to find food. Several females mate with one male. A colony nester, the males don't participate in nest building, incubation or the raising of young. Males rarely fight, but females will squabble over nest sites and materials.

AMERICAN CROW
Corvus brachyrhynchos

YEAR-ROUND

Size: 18" (45 cm)

Male: All-black bird with black bill, legs and feet. Can have purple sheen in direct sunlight.

Female: same as male

Juvenile: same as adult

Nest: platform; female builds; 1 brood per year

Eggs: 4-6; bluish to olive green, brown markings

Incubation: 18 days; female incubates

Fledging: 28-35 days; female and male feed young

Migration: non-migrator to partial migrator

Food: fruit, insects, mammals, fish, carrion, will come to seed and suet feeders

Compare: Similar to the Common Raven (pg. 25), but has a smaller bill and lacks shaggy throat feathers. Crow has higher-pitched call than the Raven's deep, low raspy call. Crow has a squared tail. Raven has a wedge-shaped tail, apparent in flight. Black-billed Magpie (pg. 47) has a long tail and white belly.

Stan's Notes: One of the most recognizable birds in Colorado. Often reuses nest every year if not taken over by a Great Horned Owl. Collects and stores bright, shiny objects in the nest. Able to mimic human voices, and other birds. One of the smartest of all birds and very social, often entertaining itself by provoking chases with other birds. Feeds on road kill but is rarely hit by cars. Can live up to 20 years. Unmated birds, known as helpers, help raise young. Large extended families roost together at night, dispersing during the day to hunt.

23

COMMON RAVEN
Corvus corax

Size: 22-27" (56-69 cm)

Male: Large all-black bird with a large black bill, a shaggy beard of feathers on the chin and throat, and a large wedge-shaped tail, seen in flight.

Female: same as male

Juvenile: same as adult

Nest: platform; female and male build; 1 brood per year

Eggs: 4-6; pale green with brown markings

Incubation: 18-21 days; female incubates

Fledging: 38-44 days; female and male feed young

Migration: non-migrator to partial migrator

Food: insects, fruit, small animals, carrion

Compare: Larger than its cousin, the American Crow (pg. 23), which lacks the throat patch of feathers. Glides on flat outstretched wings, compared to the slightly V-shaped pattern of Crow. Low raspy call distinguishes the Raven from the higher-pitched Crow.

Stan's Notes: Considered by some to be the smartest of all birds. Known for its aerial acrobatics and long swooping dives. Scavenges with crows and gulls. Known to follow wolf packs around to pick up scraps and pick at bones of a kill. Complex courtship includes grabbing bills, preening each other and cooing. Mates for life. Uses same nest site for many years. Most don't breed until 3 to 4 years of age. Much rarer Chihuahuan Raven is found in a few locations in southeastern corner of the state. Very difficult to tell them apart.

25

soaring

TURKEY VULTURE
Cathartes aura

MIGRATION
SUMMER

Size: 26-32" (66-80 cm); up to 6-foot wingspan

Male: Large bird with obvious red head and legs. In flight, the wings appear two-toned: black leading edge with gray on the trailing edge and tip. The tips of wings end in finger-like projections. Squared-off tail. Ivory bill.

Female: same as male

Juvenile: same as adult, but often a gray-to-blackish head and bill

Nest: no nest, or minimal nest on cliff or in cave; 1 brood per year

Eggs: 2; white with brown markings

Incubation: 38-41 days; female and male incubate

Fledging: 66-88 days; female and male feed young

Migration: complete, to southern states, Mexico, and Central and South America

Food: carrion, just about any dead animal of any size, parents regurgitate for young

Compare: Smaller than the Bald Eagle (pg. 55), look for Vulture's two-toned wings. Flies holding wings in a slight V shape, unlike the Eagle's straight wing position.

Stan's Notes: The vulture's naked head is an adaptation to reduce the risk of feather fouling (picking up diseases) from carcasses. Unlike hawks and eagles, it has weak feet more suited to walking than grasping. One of the few birds with a developed sense of smell. Generally mute, it makes only grunts or groans. Groups often seen in trees with wings outstretched to catch sun.

27

female pg. 109

breeding male

non-breeding male

LARK BUNTING
Calamospiza melanocorys

MIGRATION
SUMMER

Size: 6½" (16 cm)

Male: Short, stocky black bird with a large broad head, white wing patches and large bluish-gray bill. Winter is black, brown, gray and white-striped, with white wing patches.

Female: overall brown with a heavily streaked chest, a white belly, white chin flanked by black, may have dark central spot on chest

Juvenile: similar to adult of the same sex

Nest: cup; female builds; 1-2 broods per year

Eggs: 4-6; pale blue with markings

Incubation: 11-13 days; female and male incubate

Fledging: 8-12 days; female and male feed young

Migration: complete, to southwestern states, Mexico

Food: insects, seeds

Compare: The breeding male's bold black and white plumage is hard to confuse with any other bird's. Look for the rather large broad head and large bill to help identify.

Stan's Notes: The state bird of Colorado. Thought to be the fourth most numerous bird in the state. Common in eastern Colorado in the dry plains and sagebrush regions. Has short rounded wings. Flies with shallow wing beats, with the male flashing its white wing patches. Male takes to the air to display to female, setting its wings in a V position and floating back, rocking like a butterfly, singing a most amazing song. Song is like the song of Old World larks, hence the common name. Will flock with hundreds, if not thousands, of other Lark Buntings in autumn for migration.

WHITE-THROATED SWIFT
Aeronautes saxatalis

SUMMER

Size: 6½" (16 cm)

Male: Black with a white chin, chest and sides of rump. White trailing edge on the length of the first half of wings. Long narrow wings and long thin tail, as seen in flight.

Female: same as male

Juvenile: similar to adult

Nest: cup, in a cavity or crevice; female builds; 1 brood per year

Eggs: 4-5; white without markings

Incubation: unknown days; female incubates

Fledging: unknown days; female and male feed the young

Migration: complete, to Mexico and Central America

Food: insects

Compare: Similar (but not related) to the Violet-green Swallow (pg. 245), which is entirely white beneath, compared with the narrow white band on the belly of White-throated Swift.

Stan's Notes: A common bird of rocky canyons in elevations from 5,500 to 8,200 feet (1,700 to 2,500 m). A perpetual flyer, it feeds, bathes and even mates while flying. Pairs press together and spin down through air, then break apart. Flies in groups, giving twittering calls. Returns in April. Doesn't nest until summer, when more insects are available to feed to young. Carries food to the young in an expandable throat pouch. Nests in small colonies, constructing cup-shaped nests in rock crevices. Like other swifts, uses its saliva to glue feathers and vegetation into a cup that it seals to the rock.

31

male

female

DOWNY WOODPECKER
Picoides pubescens

YEAR-ROUND
WINTER

Size: 6½" (16 cm)

Male: A small woodpecker with an all-white belly, black-and-white spotted wings, a black line running through its eyes, a short black bill, a white stripe down back and a red mark on nape of neck. Several small black spots along sides of white tail.

Female: same as male, but lacks red mark on nape

Juvenile: same as female, some juveniles can have a red mark near forehead

Nest: cavity; male and female excavate; 1 brood per year

Eggs: 3-5; white without markings

Incubation: 11-12 days; female and male incubate, the female during day, male at night

Fledging: 20-25 days; male and female feed young

Migration: non-migrator

Food: insects, seeds, visits seed and suet feeders

Compare: Almost identical to the Hairy Woodpecker (pg. 39), but smaller. Look for the shorter, thinner bill of Downy to differentiate them.

Stan's Notes: Stiff tail feathers help brace this bird like a tripod as it clings to a tree. Like all woodpeckers, has long barbed tongue to pull insects from tiny places. Both sexes drum on branch or hollow log to announce territories. Male performs most brooding. Winter roosts in cavity. Two subspecies in the state; one with blacker wings with few white spots breeds in mountains, the other with extensive white spots on wings breeds in eastern Colorado (Eastern shown).

male

female

RED-NAPED SAPSUCKER
Sphyrapicus nuchalis

MIGRATION
SUMMER

Size: 8½" (22 cm)

Male: Black-and-white pattern on the back in two rows. Red forehead, chin and nape of neck.

Female: same as male, but has white chin and more white on back

Juvenile: brown version of adults, lacking any of the red markings

Nest: cavity; the male and female build; 1 brood per year

Eggs: 3-7; pale white without markings

Incubation: 12-13 days; female and male incubate

Fledging: 25-29 days; female and male feed young

Migration: complete, to Mexico and Central America

Food: insects, tree sap

Compare: Lewis's Woodpecker (pg. 249) lacks black-and-white pattern of the Red-naped. Male Williamson's Sapsucker (pg. 37) lacks the extensive red markings on head and has a bright yellow belly.

Stan's Notes: Closely related to Yellow-bellied Sapsuckers of the eastern U.S. Often associated with aspen, willow and cottonwood trees, nearly always nesting in aspens but adapting to other trees where aspens are absent. Creates several horizontal rows of holes in a tree from which sap oozes. A wide variety of birds and animals use the sap wells that sapsuckers drill. Sapsuckers lap the sap and eat the insects that are also attracted to sap. Can't suck sap as the name implies; rather, they lap it with their tongues. Some females lack the white chin that helps to differentiate the sexes.

female

male

WILLIAMSON'S SAPSUCKER
Sphyrapicus thyroideus

Size: 9" (22.5 cm)

Male: More black than white with a red chin and bright yellow belly. Bold white stripes just above and below the eyes. White rump and wing patches flash when in flight.

Female: finely barred black-and-white back with a brown head, yellow belly, no wing patches

Juvenile: similar to female

Nest: cavity; male builds; 1 brood per year

Eggs: 3-7; pale white without markings

Incubation: 12-14 days; male and female incubate

Fledging: 21-28 days; female and male feed young

Migration: complete, to Mexico and Central America

Food: insects, tree sap

Compare: Lewis's Woodpecker (pg. 249) has red face and belly. Male is similar to the Red-naped Sapsucker (pg. 35), which has white on the back and red on head. Female is similar to the Northern Flicker (pg. 147), but Flicker has a brown back and gray head.

Stan's Notes: Largest sapsucker species with a striking difference between males and females. Occupies conifer forest from 7,000 to 10,000 feet (2,150 to 3,050 m). Forages for insects and drills sap wells nearly exclusively in conifer trees. Males drum early in spring to attract mates and to claim territories. Like other sapsuckers, they have an irregular cadence to their drumming. The males excavate new cavities each year, but often in the same tree. Males do more incubating than females.

male

female

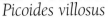

HAIRY WOODPECKER
Picoides villosus

YEAR-ROUND
WINTER

Size: 9" (22.5 cm)

Male: Black-and-white woodpecker with a white belly, and black wings with rows of white spots. White stripe down back. Long black bill. Red mark on back of head.

Female: same as male, but lacks red spot

Juvenile: grayer version of female

Nest: cavity; female and male excavate; 1 brood per year

Eggs: 3-6; white without markings

Incubation: 11-15 days; female and male incubate, the female during day, male at night

Fledging: 28-30 days; male and female feed young

Migration: non-migrator

Food: insects, nuts, seeds, comes to seed and suet feeders

Compare: Larger than Downy Woodpecker (pg. 33), Hairy has a longer bill and lacks Downy's black spots along tail.

Stan's Notes: A common backyard bird that announces its arrival with a sharp chirp before landing on feeders. Barbed tongue helps extract insects from trees. Responsible for eating many destructive forest insects. Has tiny bristle-like feathers at base of bill to protect the nostrils from wood dust. Will drum on hollow logs, branches or stovepipes in springtime to announce its territory. Often prefers to excavate nest cavities in live aspen trees. Has a larger, more oval-shaped cavity entrance than that of Downy Woodpecker.

RED-HEADED WOODPECKER
Melanerpes erythrocephalus

SUMMER

Size: 9" (22.5 cm)

Male: All-red head and a solid black back. White rump, chest and belly. Large white patches on wings flash when in flight. A black tail. Gray legs and bill.

Female: same as male

Juvenile: gray brown with white chest, lacks any red

Nest: cavity; male builds with help from female; 1 brood per year

Eggs: 4-5; white without markings

Incubation: 12-13 days; female and male incubate

Fledging: 27-30 days; female and male feed young

Migration: complete to partial migrator, moves around to areas with abundant supply of nuts

Food: insects, nuts, fruit, comes to seed and suet feeders

Compare: No other Colorado woodpecker has an all-red head.

Stan's Notes: One of the few woodpecker species in which male and female appear the same (look alike). Bill is not as well adapted for excavating holes as in other woodpeckers, so it chooses dead or rotten tree branches for nest. Prefers more open or edge woodland with many dead trees. Often seen perching on tops of dead snags. Stores acorns and other nuts.

winter

breeding

AMERICAN AVOCET
Recurvirostra americana

Size: 18" (45 cm)

Male: Black and white back, white belly. A long, thin upturned bill and long gray legs. Head and neck rusty red during breeding, gray in the winter.

Female: similar to male, only with a more strongly upturned bill

Juvenile: similar to adults, with a slight wash of rusty red on neck and head

Nest: ground; the female and male build; 1 brood per year

Eggs: 3-5; light olive with brown markings

Incubation: 22-29 days; female and male incubate

Fledging: 28-35 days; female and male feed young

Migration: complete, to southwestern states, Mexico

Food: insects, crustaceans, aquatic vegetation and fruit

Compare: One of the few long-legged shorebirds in Colorado. Look for the obvious rusty head of breeding Avocet and long upturned bill.

Stan's Notes: A handsome long-legged bird that prefers shallow alkaline, saline or brackish water. Uses its up-curved bill to sweep from side to side across mud bottoms in search of insects. Both the male and female have a brood patch to incubate eggs and brood young. Nests in loose colonies of up to 20 pairs. All members of the colony will defend together against intruders. Nests in eastern half of the state.

male

female pg. 155

COMMON GOLDENEYE
Bucephala clangula

WINTER

Size: 18½-20" (47-50 cm)

Male: A mostly white duck with a black back, a large, puffy green head and a large white spot in front of each bright golden eye. Dark bill.

Female: brown and gray, a large dark brown head, gray body, white collar, bright golden eyes, yellow-tipped dark bill

Juvenile: same as female, but has a dark bill

Nest: cavity; female lines old woodpecker cavity; 1 brood per year

Eggs: 8-10; light green without markings

Incubation: 28-32 days; female incubates

Fledging: 56-59 days; female leads young to food

Migration: complete, to southern states

Food: aquatic plants, insects

Compare: Larger than American Coot (pg. 19), which lacks the bright golden eyes and white spot in front of each eye.

Stan's Notes: Known for their loud whistling, which is produced by their wings in flight. In late winter and early spring, males often attract females through elaborate displays, throwing their heads backward while uttering a single raspy note. Females will lay eggs in other goldeneye nests, resulting in some mothers incubating up to 30 eggs. Received its common name from its obvious bright golden eyes.

BLACK-BILLED MAGPIE
Pica hudsonia

YEAR-ROUND

Size: 20" (50 cm)

Male: A large black-and-white bird with very long tail and white belly. Iridescent green wings and tail in direct sunlight. Large black bill and legs. White wing patches flash in flight.

Female: same as male

Juvenile: same as adult, but shorter tail

Nest: modified pendulous; the female and male build; 1 brood per year

Eggs: 5-8; green with brown markings

Incubation: 16-21 days; female incubates

Fledging: 25-29 days; female and male feed young

Migration: non-migrator

Food: insects, carrion, fruit, seeds

Compare: Larger than the Common Grackle (pg. 17). Contrasting black-and-white colors and the very long tail of Magpie distinguish it from the all-black American Crow (pg. 23).

Stan's Notes: A wonderfully intelligent bird that will often raid a barnyard dog dish for food. Travels in small flocks usually made up of family members and tends to be very gregarious. Breeds in small colonies with unusual dome nest (dome-shaped roof) deep within thick shrubs. Will mate with same mate for several years. Able to mimic dogs, cats and even people. Prefers open fields with cattle or sheep, where it feeds upon insects attracted to the livestock.

BLACK-CROWNED NIGHT-HERON
Nycticorax nycticorax

YEAR-ROUND
MIGRATION
SUMMER

Size: 22-27" (56-69 cm)

Male: A stocky, hunched and inactive heron with black back and crown, white belly and gray wings. Long dark bill, short yellow legs and bright red eyes. Breeding adult has two long white crown plumes.

Female: same as male

Juvenile: golden brown head and back with white spots, streaked breast, yellow orange eyes, brown bill

Nest: platform; female and male build; 1 brood per year

Eggs: 3-5; light blue without markings

Incubation: 24-26 days; female and male incubate

Fledging: 42-48 days; female and male feed young

Migration: complete, to southern states, Mexico and Central America

Food: fish, aquatic insects

Compare: Half the size of Great Blue Heron (pg. 239) when perching. Look for a short-necked heron with a black back and crown.

Stan's Notes: A very secretive bird, this heron is most active near dawn and dusk. Hunts alone, but nests in small colonies. Roosts in trees during the day. Often squawks when disturbed from daytime roost. Often seen being harassed by other herons during the day.

rushing

weed dance

WESTERN GREBE
Aechmophorus occidentalis

SUMMER

Size: 24" (60 cm)

Male: A long-necked, nearly all-black water bird with a white throat. Long yellow bill with bright red eyes. Dark cap extends around eyes to base of bill. During winter, becomes light gray around eyes.

Female: same as male

Juvenile: similar to adult

Nest: platform; female and male build; 1 brood per year

Eggs: 3-4; bluish white with brown markings

Incubation: 20-23 days; female and male incubate

Fledging: 65-75 days; female and male feed young

Migration: complete, to coastal California and Mexico

Food: fish, aquatic insects

Compare: A familiar long-necked water bird. Striking black and white plumage makes it hard to confuse with any other bird.

Stan's Notes: Well known for its unusual breeding dance known as rushing. Side by side, with necks outstretched, mates will spring to their webbed feet and dance across the water's surface (see inset), diving underwater at the end of the rush. Often holds long stalks of water plants in bill when courting mate, called the weed dance (see inset). Its legs are positioned far back on the body, making it difficult to walk on ground. Shortly after choosing a large lake for breeding and till late in summer, it rarely flies. Young ride on backs of adults, climbing on only minutes after hatching. Nests in large colonies of up to 100 pairs on lakes with lots of tall vegetation.

soaring

OSPREY
Pandion haliaetus

Size: 24" (60 cm); up to 6-foot wingspan

Male: Large eagle-like bird with white chest, belly and black brown back. White head with a black streak across eyes. Large wings with black "wrist" marks.

Female: same as male, but with a necklace of brown streaking

Juvenile: similar to adults, with a light tan breast

Nest: platform; female and male build; 1 brood per year

Eggs: 2-4; white with brown markings

Incubation: 32-42 days; female and male incubate

Fledging: 48-58 days; male and female feed young

Migration: complete, to Mexico, Central America and South America

Food: fish

Compare: Bald Eagle (pg. 55) is on average 10 inches (25 cm) larger, with an all-white head and tail. The juvenile Bald Eagle is brown with white speckles. Look for a white belly and dark stripe across eyes to identify Osprey.

Stan's Notes: Ospreys are in a family all their own. It is the only raptor that will plunge into the water to catch fish. Can hover for several seconds before diving. Carries fish in a head-first position during flight for better aerodynamics. In flight, wings are angled (cocked) backward. Nests on man-made towers and tall dead trees. Recent studies show that male and female might mate for life, but don't migrate to the same wintering grounds.

soaring

juvenile

BALD EAGLE
Haliaeetus leucocephalus

YEAR-ROUND
SUMMER
WINTER

Size: 31-37" (79-94 cm); up to 7-foot wingspan

Male: Pure white head and tail contrast with dark brown-to-black body and wings. A large, curved yellow bill and yellow feet.

Female: same as male, only slightly larger

Juvenile: dark brown with white spots or speckles throughout body and wings, gray bill

Nest: massive platform; female and male build; 1 brood per year

Eggs: 2; off-white without markings

Incubation: 34-36 days; female and male incubate

Fledging: 75-90 days; female and male feed young

Migration: partial migrator, to southeastern states

Food: fish, carrion, ducks

Compare: Golden Eagle (pg. 175) and Turkey Vulture (pg. 27) lack the white head and white tail of adult Bald Eagle. Juvenile Golden Eagle, with its white wrist marks and white base of tail, is similar to the juvenile Bald Eagle.

Stan's Notes: Often seen soaring, this bird is making a comeback in Colorado. Returns to same nest every year, adding more sticks, enlarging it to massive proportions, at times up to 1,000 pounds (450 kg). In the midair mating ritual, one bird flips upside down, locking talons with another. Both tumble until they break apart to continue flying. Thought to mate for life, but will switch mates if not successful reproducing. Juveniles attain the white head and tail at about 4 to 5 years of age.

BLUE-GRAY GNATCATCHER
Polioptila caerulea

MIGRATION
SUMMER

Size: 4" (10 cm)

Male: A light blue-to-gray head, back, breast and wings, with a black forehead and eyebrows. White belly and prominent white eye-ring. Long black tail with a white undertail, often held cocked above the rest of body.

Female: same as male, only grayer and lacking black on head

Juvenile: similar to female

Nest: cup; female and male build; 1 brood a year

Eggs: 4-5; pale blue with dark markings

Incubation: 10-13 days; female and male incubate

Fledging: 10-12 days; female and male feed young

Migration: complete, to southern states, the Bahamas, Mexico and Central America

Food: insects

Compare: The only small blue bird with a black tail. Constantly flicks its tail up and down and from side to side. Very active near the nest, look for it flitting around upper branches in search of insects.

Stan's Notes: Found in a wide variety of forest types throughout most of Colorado. Has been increasing and expanding its range northward along the eastern slope of the Rockies over the past few decades. Listen for its wheezy call notes to help locate. A fun and easy bird to watch as it cocks and fans tail while calling. Like many open woodland nesters, it is a common cowbird host. Returns to Colorado by mid-April, with most leaving by the end of August.

TREE SWALLOW
Tachycineta bicolor

Size: 5-6" (13-15 cm)

Male: Blue green in the spring and greener in fall. Appears to change color in direct sunlight. A white belly, a notched tail and pointed wing tips.

Female: similar to male, only duller

Juvenile: gray brown with a white belly and grayish breast band

Nest: cavity; female and male line former woodpecker cavity or nest box; 1 brood per year

Eggs: 4-6; white without markings

Incubation: 13-16 days; female incubates

Fledging: 20-24 days; female and male feed young

Migration: complete, to Mexico and Central America

Food: insects

Compare: Barn Swallow (pg. 69) has a rust belly and deeply forked tail. Similar size as the Cliff Swallow (pg. 93) and Violet-green Swallow (pg. 245), but lacks any tan-to-rust color of the Cliff Swallow and any emerald green of the Violet-green Swallow.

Stan's Notes: The first swallow species to return each spring. Most common along ponds, lakes and agricultural fields. Is attracted to your yard with a nest box. Competes with Western and Mountain Bluebirds for cavities and nest boxes. Travels great distances to find dropped feathers to line its grass nest. Sometimes seen playing, chasing after dropped feathers. Often seen flying back and forth across fields, feeding on insects. Gathers in large flocks to migrate.

female pg. 91

male

LAZULI BUNTING
Passerina amoena

SUMMER

Size: 5½" (14 cm)

Male: A turquoise blue head, neck, back and tail. Cinnamon chest with cinnamon extending down flanks slightly. White belly. Two bold white wing bars. Non-breeding male has a spotty blue head and back.

Female: overall grayish brown, warm-brown breast, a light wash of blue on wings and tail, gray throat, a light gray belly, two narrow white wing bars

Juvenile: similar to adult of the same sex

Nest: cup; female builds; 2-3 broods per year

Eggs: 3-5; pale blue without markings

Incubation: 11-13 days; female incubates

Fledging: 10-12 days; female and male feed young

Migration: complete, to Mexico

Food: insects, seeds

Compare: Smaller than the male Western Bluebird (pg. 67), not as dark blue in color and chest is browner. Male Blue Grosbeak (pg. 63) has chestnut wing bars and lacks the male Bunting's white belly.

Stan's Notes: More common in shrub lands between 5,000 and 7,000 feet (1,500 to 2,150 m) in western half of Colorado. Strong association with water such as rivers and streams. Has increased in populations and also expanded its range eastward over the last 100 years. After breeding, gathers in small flocks and tends to move up in elevations to hunt for insects and search for seeds.

female pg. 117

male

BLUE GROSBEAK
Passerina caerulea

SUMMER

Size: 7" (18 cm)

Male: An overall blue bird. Two chestnut-colored wing bars. A large gray-to-silver bill, black around base of bill.

Female: overall brown with darker wings and tail, two tan wing bars, large gray-to-silver bill

Juvenile: similar to female

Nest: cup; female builds; 1-2 broods per year

Eggs: 3-6; pale blue without markings

Incubation: 11-12 days; female incubates

Fledging: 9-10 days; female and male feed young

Migration: complete, to Central America, the Bahamas, Cuba and Mexico

Food: insects, seeds, will come to seed feeders

Compare: Male Lazuli Bunting (pg. 61) has two bold white wing bars and a white belly. The male Mountain and Western Bluebirds (pp. 65 and 67, respectively) are the same size, but lack the male Grosbeak's chestnut-colored wing bars and oversized bill.

Stan's Notes: Blue Grosbeaks return to the state late, by mid-May. Most common in southeastern Colorado, but expanding northward with overall populations increasing over the past 30 to 40 years. A bird of semi-open habitats such as overgrown fields, riversides and woodland edges. Often seen twitching and spreading its tail. First-year males show only some blue, obtaining the full complement of blue feathers in the second winter. Will come to seed feeders.

male

female

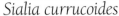

MOUNTAIN BLUEBIRD
Sialia currucoides

YEAR-ROUND
MIGRATION
SUMMER

Size: 7" (18 cm)

Male: An overall sky blue with darker blue back, wings, tail and head.

Female: similar to male, only paler with nearly gray head, chest and white belly

Juvenile: similar to adult of the same sex

Nest: cavity, old woodpecker cavity, wooden nest box; female builds; 1-2 broods per year

Eggs: 4-6; pale blue without markings

Incubation: 13-14 days; female incubates

Fledging: 22-23 days; female and male feed young

Migration: complete, southwestern states and Mexico, non-migrator in parts of Colorado

Food: insects

Compare: Similar to Western Bluebird (pg. 67), but not as dark blue and lacks Western's rusty red chest. Same size as male Blue Grosbeak (pg. 63), but lacks the Grosbeak's chestnut-colored wing bars and oversized bill.

Stan's Notes: Common in open mountainous country, nesting in the western two-thirds of the state. Due to conservation of suitable nesting sites (dead trees with cavities and man-made nest boxes), populations have increased dramatically. Like the other bluebirds, Mountain Bluebirds take well to nest boxes and will tolerate close contact with humans. Young will imprint on their first nest box or cavity, then choose a similar type of box or cavity throughout the rest of life.

male

female

WESTERN BLUEBIRD
Sialia mexicana

YEAR-ROUND
MIGRATION
SUMMER
WINTER

Size: 7" (18 cm)

Male: Deep blue head, neck, back, wings and tail. Rusty red chest and flanks.

Female: similar to male, only duller with gray head

Juvenile: similar to female, with a speckled chest

Nest: cavity, old woodpecker cavity, wooden nest box; female builds; 1-2 broods per year

Eggs: 4-6; pale blue without markings

Incubation: 13-14 days; female incubates

Fledging: 22-23 days; female and male feed young

Migration: complete, southwestern states and Mexico, non-migrator in parts of Colorado

Food: insects, fruit

Compare: Mountain Bluebird (pg. 65) is similar, but lacks the rusty red breast. Larger than male Lazuli Bunting (pg. 61), which has white wing bars. Same size as male Blue Grosbeak (pg. 63), but lacks the Grosbeak's chestnut wing bars and oversized bill.

Stan's Notes: Not as common and widespread as the Mountain Bluebird. Mostly found on both fronts of the Rocky Mountains in Ponderosa Pine forest between elevations of 5,000 and 8,000 feet (1,500 to 2,450 m). Like Mountain Bluebirds, Western Bluebirds use nest boxes, which are responsible for the stable populations. Courting male will fly in front of female, spreading wings and tail, then perch next to her. Often seen going in and out of nest box or cavity as if to say, "Look inside." Male may offer food to female to establish pair bond.

BARN SWALLOW
Hirundo rustica

Size: 7" (18 cm)

Male: A sleek swallow with a blue black back, a cinnamon belly and a reddish brown chin. White spots on long forked tail.

Female: same as male, only slightly duller

Juvenile: similar to adults, with a tan belly and chin, and shorter tail

Nest: cup; female and male build; 2 broods a year

Eggs: 4-5; white with brown markings

Incubation: 13-17 days; female incubates

Fledging: 18-23 days; female and male feed young

Migration: complete, to South America

Food: insects, prefers beetles, wasps and flies

Compare: Tree Swallow (pg. 59) has a white belly and chin, and notched tail. Larger than the Cliff Swallow (pg. 93) and Violet-green Swallow (pg. 245), which both lack the distinctive, deeply forked tail. Violet-green Swallow is distinctively green with a white face.

Stan's Notes: Of the seven swallow species in Colorado, this is the only one with a deeply forked tail. Unlike other swallows, the Barn Swallow rarely glides in flight, so look for continuous flapping. It builds a mud nest using up to 1,000 beak-loads of mud, often in or on barns. Nests in colonies of four to six, but nesting alone is not uncommon. Drinks while flying by skimming water or getting water from wet leaves. It also bathes while flying through the rain or sprinklers.

STELLER'S JAY
Cyanocitta stelleri

YEAR-ROUND

Size: 11" (28 cm)

Male: Dark blue wings, tail and belly. Black head, nape of the neck and chest. Large, pointed black crest on head that can be lifted at will. Distinctive white streaks on forehead and just above eyes.

Female: same as male

Juvenile: similar to adult, lacking white markings on forehead and eye stripe

Nest: cup; female and male build; 1 brood a year

Eggs: 3-5; pale green with brown markings

Incubation: 14-16 days; female incubates

Fledging: 16-18 days; female and male feed young

Migration: non-migrator

Food: insects, berries, seeds, will visit seed feeders

Compare: Slightly smaller than the Blue Jay (pg. 73), which lacks the distinctive black head and crest of Steller's Jay. The Gray Jay (pg. 215) lacks any blue coloring and a crest.

Stan's Notes: Common resident of foothills and lower mountains from 6,000 to 8,000 feet (1,850 to 2,450 m). Usually only found in conifer forest, it rarely competes with Blue Jays, which occupy territories in lower elevations, and Gray Jays, which occupy higher elevations. Thought to mate for life, rarely dispersing far, usually breeding within 10 miles (16 km) of the place of birth. Several sub-species found throughout the Rockies. Colorado form has a black crest with distinct white streaks, while others lack white markings.

71

BLUE JAY
Cyanocitta cristata

YEAR-ROUND

Size: 12" (30 cm)

Male: Large bright-light-blue and white bird with black necklace. Crest moves up and down at will. White face with a gray belly. White wing bars on blue wings. Black spots and a white tip on blue tail.

Female: same as male

Juvenile: same as adult, only duller

Nest: cup; the female and male build; 1-2 broods per year

Eggs: 4-5; green to blue with brown markings

Incubation: 16-18 days; female incubates

Fledging: 17-21 days; female and male feed young

Migration: non-migrator to partial migrator, will move around to find abundant food source

Food: insects, fruit, carrion, seeds, nuts, attracted to seed feeders

Compare: Steller's Jay (pg. 71) is smaller, with a black head and a large crest. Gray Jay (pg. 215) lacks any blue coloring. Kingfisher (pg. 75) lacks a vivid blue color and black necklace.

Stan's Notes: Highly intelligent bird, solving problems, gathering food and communicating more than other birds. Will scream like a hawk to scatter birds at a feeder before approaching. Known as the alarm of the forest, screaming at any intruders in the woods. Is known to eat eggs or young birds from nests of other birds. One of the few birds to cache food. Feathers don't have blue pigment; refracted sunlight casts blue light.

male

female

BELTED KINGFISHER
Ceryle alcyon

YEAR-ROUND
SUMMER

Size: 13" (33 cm)

Male: Large blue bird with white belly. Broad blue gray breast band and a ragged crest that is raised and lowered at will. Large head with a long, thick black bill. A small white spot directly in front of red brown eyes. Black wing tips with splashes of white that flash when flying.

Female: same as male, but with rusty breast band in addition to blue gray band, and rusty flanks

Juvenile: similar to female

Nest: cavity; female and male excavate; 1 brood per year

Eggs: 6-7; white without markings

Incubation: 23-24 days; female and male incubate

Fledging: 23-24 days; female and male feed young

Migration: complete, to southern states, Mexico, and Central and South America

Food: small fish

Compare: Similar in size to the Blue Jay (pg. 73), but Kingfisher is darker blue with larger, more ragged crest.

Stan's Notes: Seen perched on branches near the water, it dives headfirst for small fish and returns to a branch to eat. Has a loud machine-gun-like call. Excavates a deep cavity in bank of river or lake. Parents drop dead fish into water, teaching young to dive. Regurgitates pellets of bone after meals, being unable to pass bones through digestive tract. Mates recognize each other by call.

BROWN CREEPER
Certhia americana

YEAR-ROUND
MIGRATION
WINTER

Size: 5" (13 cm)

Male: Small, thin, nearly camouflaged brown bird. White from chin to belly. White eyebrows. Long stiff tail. Dark eyes. Thin curved bill.

Female: same as male

Juvenile: same as adult

Nest: cup; female builds; unknown how many broods per year

Eggs: 5-6; white with tiny brown markings

Incubation: 14-17 days; female incubates, male feeds female during incubation

Fledging: 13-16 days; female and male feed young

Migration: partial migrator to non-migrator

Food: insects, nuts, seeds

Compare: Creeps up tree trunks, not down, like the White-breasted Nuthatch (pg. 191). Watch for Creeper to fly from the top of one trunk to the bottom of another, working its way to the top, looking for insects. Slightly larger than the Red-breasted Nuthatch (pg. 183), with a similar white stripe above eyes, but Creeper has a white belly, long tail and no black crown.

Stan's Notes: Utilizes its camouflage coloring to defend itself by spreading out flat on a branch or tree trunk without moving. The young are able to follow the parents, creeping soon after fledging. Commonly seen in wooded areas. Often builds nest behind loose bark of dead or dying trees.

HOUSE WREN
Troglodytes aedon

Size: 5" (13 cm)

Male: A small all-brown bird with lighter brown marking on tail and wings. Brown, slightly curved bill. Often holds its tail erect.

Female: same as male

Juvenile: same as adult

Nest: cavity; female and male line just about any cavity; 2 broods per year

Eggs: 4-6; tan with brown markings

Incubation: 10-13 days; female and male incubate

Fledging: 12-15 days; female and male feed young

Migration: complete, to southern states and Mexico

Food: insects

Compare: The Canyon Wren (pg. 95) and Rock Wren (pg. 97) are slightly larger. House Wren lacks the distinctive white throat and chest of Canyon Wren and a long down-curved bill. Rock Wren has fine white speckles on the back with a light tan belly and chest.

Stan's Notes: A prolific songster, it will sing from dawn until dusk during the mating season. Easily attracted to nest boxes. In spring, the male chooses several prospective nesting cavities and places a few small twigs in each. Female inspects each, chooses one, and finishes the nest building. She will completely fill the nest cavity with uniformly small twigs, then line a small depression at back of cavity with pine needles and grass. Often has trouble fitting long twigs through nest cavity hole. Tries many different directions and approaches until successful.

PINE SISKIN
Carduelis pinus

YEAR-ROUND
WINTER

Size: 5" (13 cm)

Male: A small brown finch with heavily streaked back, breast and belly. Yellow wing bars and yellow at base of tail. Thin bill.

Female: same as male

Juvenile: similar to adult, with a light yellow tinge throughout chest and chin

Nest: modified cup; the female builds; 2 broods per year

Eggs: 3-4; greenish blue with brown markings

Incubation: 12-13 days; female incubates

Fledging: 14-15 days; female and male feed young

Migration: irruptive, moves around the state in search of food

Food: seeds, insects, will come to seed feeders

Compare: The female American Goldfinch (pg. 289) lacks the streaks and has white wing bars. The female House Finch (pg. 83) shares a streaked chest, but lacks yellow wing bars.

Stan's Notes: A nesting resident, it is usually considered a winter finch because it is more visible in the non-nesting season, when it gathers in flocks, moves around the state and visits bird feeders. Nests in the western half of Colorado, with nests often only a few feet apart. Builds nest toward the ends of conifer branches, where the needles are dense, helping to conceal. Breeds in small groups. Male feeds female during incubation. Juveniles lose yellow tint on chest and chin by late summer of first year.

female

male pg. 265

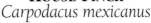

HOUSE FINCH
Carpodacus mexicanus

YEAR-ROUND

Size: 5" (13 cm)

Female: A plain brown bird with a heavily streaked white chest.

Male: orange red face, chest and rump, a brown cap, brown marking behind eyes, brown wings streaked with white, streaked belly

Juvenile: similar to female

Nest: cup, sometimes in cavities; female builds; 2 broods per year

Eggs: 4-5; pale blue, lightly marked

Incubation: 12-14 days; female incubates

Fledging: 15-19 days; female and male feed young

Migration: non-migrator to partial migrator, will move around to find food

Food: seeds, fruit, leaf buds, will visit seed feeders

Compare: Female Cassin's Finch (pg. 107) has a more heavily streaked belly. Similar to Pine Siskin (pg. 81), but lacks yellow wing bars and has larger bill. Female Goldfinch (pg. 289) has a clear chest and white wing bars.

Stan's Notes: Very social bird. Visits feeders in small flocks. Likes nesting in hanging flower baskets. Incubating female fed by male. Loud, cheerful warbling song. Suffers a fatal eye disease that causes eyes to crust over. Historically it occurred from the Pacific coast to the Rockies, with only a few reaching the eastern side. Now found all over Colorado. Unknown if birds east of mountains came from the west or are from eastern birds introduced to Long Island, New York, in the 1940s, which have populated the entire eastern U.S.

CHIPPING SPARROW
Spizella passerina

Size: 5" (13 cm)

Male: Small gray brown sparrow with a clear gray chest, rusty crown, white eyebrows with a black eye line, thin gray black bill and two faint wing bars.

Female: same as male

Juvenile: similar to adult, but has streaked chest and lacks rusty cap

Nest: cup; female builds; 2 broods per year

Eggs: 3-5; blue green with brown markings

Incubation: 11-14 days; female incubates

Fledging: 10-12 days; female and male feed young

Migration: complete, to southern states, Mexico and Central America

Food: insects, seeds, will come to ground feeders

Compare: Similar to American Tree Sparrow (pg. 99), which shares a rusty crown, but lacks dark eye line. Lark Sparrow (pg. 111) is larger, with a white chest and central spot. Smaller than the Song Sparrow (pg. 87), which has a heavily streaked chest. The female House Finch (pg. 83) also has a streaked chest.

Stan's Notes: A common garden or yard bird, often seen feeding on dropped seeds below feeders. Gathers in large family groups to feed each autumn in preparation for migration. Migrates at night in flocks of 20 to 30 birds. Received its common name from the male's slow "chip" call. Often just called Chippy. Nest is placed low in dense shrubs and is almost always lined with animal hair.

SONG SPARROW
Melospiza melodia

Size: 5-6" (13-15 cm)

Male: Common brown sparrow with heavy dark streaks on breast coalescing into a central dark spot.

Female: same as male

Juvenile: similar to adult, finely streaked chest without central spot

Nest: cup; female builds; 2 broods per year

Eggs: 3-4; pale blue to green with reddish brown markings

Incubation: 12-14 days; female incubates

Fledging: 9-12 days; female and male feed young

Migration: complete, to southern states, non-migrator in parts of Colorado

Food: insects, seeds, rarely visits seed feeders

Compare: Similar to other brown sparrows. Look for a heavily streaked chest with central dark spot.

Stan's Notes: Many Song Sparrow subspecies or varieties, but dark central spot carries through each variant. While the female builds another nest for second brood, the male often takes over feeding the young. Returns to similar area each year, defending a small territory by singing from thick shrubs. Common host of the Brown-headed Cowbird. Ground feeders, look for them to scratch simultaneously with both feet to expose seeds. Unlike many sparrow species, Song Sparrows rarely flock together.

male pg. 189

female

gray-headed

Oregon female

DARK-EYED JUNCO
Junco hyemalis

YEAR-ROUND
WINTER

Size: 5½" (14 cm)

Female: A round, dark-eyed bird with tan-to-brown chest, head and back. White belly. Ivory-to-pink bill. Since the outermost tail feathers are white, tail appears as a white V in flight.

Male: same as female, only slate gray to charcoal

Juvenile: similar to female, but has a streaked breast and head

Nest: cup; female and male build; 2 broods a year

Eggs: 3-5; white with reddish brown markings

Incubation: 12-13 days; female incubates

Fledging: 10-13 days; male and female feed young

Migration: partial migrator to complete, across the U.S.

Food: seeds, insects, will come to seed feeders

Compare: Rarely confused with any other bird. Large flocks come to feed under bird feeders.

Stan's Notes: Several junco species have now been combined into one, simply called Dark-eyed Junco (see inset photos). Estimates of over 2 million juncos found in Colorado, making it one of the most numerous breeding birds in the state. Common year-round bird of Colorado, spending winters in foothills and plains after snowmelt, returning to higher elevations for nesting. Nests in a wide variety of wooded habitats in April and May. Usually seen on the ground in small flocks. It adheres to a rigid social hierarchy, with dominant birds chasing the less dominant birds. Look for its white outer tail feathers flashing in flight. Most comfortable on the ground, juncos will "double-scratch" with both feet to expose seeds and insects. Consumes many weed seeds.

male pg. 61

female

LAZULI BUNTING
Passerina amoena

SUMMER

Size:	5½" (14 cm)
Female:	Overall grayish brown with a warm-brown chest, light wash of blue on wings and tail, gray throat and light gray belly. Two narrow white wing bars.
Male:	turquoise blue head, neck, back and tail, cinnamon chest, white belly and two bold white wing bars
Juvenile:	similar to adult of the same sex
Nest:	cup; female builds; 2-3 broods per year
Eggs:	3-5; pale blue without markings
Incubation:	11-13 days; female incubates
Fledging:	10-12 days; female and male feed young
Migration:	complete, to Mexico
Food:	insects, seeds
Compare:	Similar to female Blue Grosbeak (pg. 117), which is overall darker and has tan wing bars. Female Mountain Bluebird (pg. 65) and Western Bluebird (pg. 67) are larger, with both showing much more blue than the female Bunting.

Stan's Notes: More common in shrub lands between 5,000 and 7,000 feet (1,500 to 2,150 m) in western half of Colorado. Strong association with water such as rivers and streams. Has increased in populations and also expanded its range eastward over the last 100 years. After breeding, gathers in small flocks and tends to move up in elevations to hunt for insects and search for seeds.

CLIFF SWALLOW
Petrochelidon pyrrhonota

Size: 5½" (14 cm)

Male: A uniquely patterned swallow with a dark back, wings and cap. Distinctive tan-to-rust rump, cheeks and forehead.

Female: same as male

Juvenile: similar to adult, lacks distinct patterning

Nest: gourd-shaped, made of mud; the male and female build; 1-2 broods per year

Eggs: 3-6; pale white with brown markings

Incubation: 14-16 days; male and female incubate

Fledging: 21-24 days; female and male feed young

Migration: complete, to South America

Food: insects

Compare: Smaller than Barn Swallow (pg. 69), which has a blue back and wings, and a deeply forked tail. The Tree Swallow (pg. 59) lacks any tan-to-rust coloring. The Violet-green Swallow (pg. 245) is green with a bright white face.

Stan's Notes: Considered the most abundant swallow species in Colorado. Common around bridges and rural housing, especially in open country near cliffs. Builds gourd-shaped nest with funnel-like entrance pointing down. Colony nester, with many nests lined up under eaves of buildings or under cliff overhangs. Will carry balls of mud up to a mile to construct nest. Many of the colony return to the same nest sites every year. Not unusual to have two broods per season. If the number of nests under eaves becomes a problem, wait until after young have left the nests to hose off the mud.

CANYON WREN
Catherpes mexicanus

YEAR-ROUND

Size: 5¾" (14.5 cm)

Male: Chestnut back, wings, belly and tail. Gray head and nape of neck. A distinctive white throat and chest. Long downward-curving bill. Tail often cocked up.

Female: same as male

Juvenile: similar to adult

Nest: crevice; male and female build; 1-2 broods per year

Eggs: 4-6; white with light brown markings

Incubation: 14-16 days; female and male incubate

Fledging: 14-18 days; female and male feed young

Migration: non-migrator to partial migrator

Food: insects

Compare: Slightly smaller than Rock Wren (pg. 97), which tends to be more grayish with white chin not as prominent. Slightly larger than the House Wren (pg. 79), which lacks the large bill of the Canyon Wren.

Stan's Notes: An active wren, spending its entire life among rocks and cliffs. Prefers steep-sided canyons, hence its common name. Maintains winter territories, usually around running water, to hunt for winter-active insects. Territories are up to 2 acres (1 ha) in size. Nests are attached to rocks within crevices that usually have some kind of rock covering. May reuse the nest from year to year. Lives in close association with Rock Wrens, which use scattered boulders and rocks for nesting.

ROCK WREN
Salpinctes obsoletus

MIGRATION
SUMMER

Size: 6" (15 cm)

Male: Overall grayish brown with tinges of buff brown on tail and wings. Gray back often finely speckled with white. Belly and chest are light tan.

Female: same as male

Juvenile: similar to adult

Nest: crevice; male and female build; 1-2 broods per year

Eggs: 4-8; white with light brown markings

Incubation: 14-16 days; female and male incubate

Fledging: 14-18 days; female and male feed young

Migration: complete, to southern states

Food: insects

Compare: Slightly larger than Canyon Wren (pg. 95), which has a much larger and down-curved bill and is mostly chestnut brown. Slightly larger than the House Wren (pg. 79).

Stan's Notes: Consistently uses open sunny piles of broken rocks (scree) and rock debris at cliff bases (talus slopes) for nesting. Often builds a small runway of flat stones leading up to the nest, which is usually in a rock crevice. Lives in close association with Canyon Wrens, which use steep-sided canyons for nesting. Known to also nest on prairies, where it uses dirt banks instead of rock piles. The female does most of the incubating, with the male feeding female during incubation.

side view

front view

AMERICAN TREE SPARROW
Spizella arborea

MIGRATION
WINTER

Size: 6" (15 cm)

Male: A common brown sparrow with tan breast and rusty crown. Note single black spot in center of the breast. Upper bill dark, lower bill yellow. Two white wing bars and a gray eye stripe.

Female: same as male

Juvenile: lacks rusty crown, has streaked chest, often obscuring the central dark spot

Nest: cup; female builds; 1 brood per year

Eggs: 3-5; green white with brown markings

Incubation: 12-13 days; female incubates

Fledging: 8-10 days; female and male feed young

Migration: complete, throughout North America

Food: insects, seeds, occasionally visits feeders

Compare: Looks similar to other sparrows, so look closely at the center of the breast for the single dark spot. Shares a rusty crown with the Chipping Sparrow (pg. 85), but lacks Chippy's distinctive white eyebrows and black eye line. Song Sparrow (pg. 87) has a heavily streaked chest.

Stan's Notes: Commonly seen during spring and fall migrations in small flocks of 2 to 200. A regular winter bird feeder visitor in eastern parts of Colorado. Sometimes called Winter Chippy since it looks similar to the Chipping Sparrow, a summer visitor. Nests in northern Canada and Alaska.

HOUSE SPARROW
Passer domesticus

YEAR-ROUND

Size: 6" (15 cm)

Male: Medium sparrow-like bird with large black spot on throat extending down to the chest. Brown back and single white wing bars. A gray belly and crown.

Female: all-light-brown bird, slightly smaller, lacks the black throat patch and single wing bars

Juvenile: similar to female

Nest: domed cup nest, within cavity; female and male build; 2-3 broods per year

Eggs: 4-6; white with brown markings

Incubation: 10-12 days; female incubates

Fledging: 14-17 days; female and male feed young

Migration: non-migrator, moves around to find food

Food: seeds, insects, fruit, comes to seed feeders

Compare: Lacks the rusty crown of the American Tree Sparrow (pg. 99) and Chipping Sparrow (pg. 85). Look for male House Sparrow's black bib. Female has a clear breast and no marking on head (cap).

Stan's Notes: One of the first bird songs heard in cities in spring. Familiar city bird, nearly always in flocks. Introduced from Europe to Central Park, New York, in 1850 and now found throughout North America. These birds are not really sparrows, but members of the Weaver Finch family, characterized by their large, oversized domed nests. Constructs a nest containing scraps of plastic, paper and whatever else is available. An aggressive bird that will kill the young of other birds in order to take over a cavity.

male

female

BROWN-CAPPED ROSY-FINCH
Leucosticte australis

YEAR-ROUND
WINTER

Size: 6" (15 cm)

Male: An overall warm brown with a dark brown cap and extensive rosy red on wings, rump and belly. Tiny white patch at base of a dark upper bill.

Female: same as male, but has less pink

Juvenile: similar to adults, but a light gray, lacks rosy red color and has a yellow bill

Nest: cup; female builds; 1-2 broods per year

Eggs: 3-5; white without markings

Incubation: 12-14 days; female incubates

Fledging: 16-18 days; female and male feed young

Migration: partial migrator to non-migrator, will move around in higher elevations to find food

Food: seeds, insects, will visit seed feeders

Compare: Similar to the Black Rosy-Finch (pg. 3) and Gray-crowned Rosy-Finch (pg. 105), but is a rich warm brown with little or no gray on the head.

Stan's Notes: Found in high alpine regions, nesting in steep cliff faces. Year-round resident, breeding in high rocky elevations. One of the few species in which the females determine territories and choose nest sites. Consequently, the male has a poorly developed song because it doesn't need it to attract mates or defend territories. During breeding, both male and female develop an opening in the floor of the mouth (buccal pouch), used for carrying a large supply of food, such as insects, to the young in the nest.

male

female

GRAY-CROWNED ROSY-FINCH
Leucosticte tephrocotis

WINTER

Size: 6" (15 cm)

Male: Gray crown with a black forehead, chin and throat. Warm cinnamon-brown body with a wash of rosy red, especially along flanks and rump.

Female: same as male, but has less pink

Juvenile: similar to adult of the same sex

Nest: cup; female builds; 1-2 broods per year

Eggs: 3-5; white without markings

Incubation: 12-14 days; female incubates

Fledging: 16-18 days; female and male feed young

Migration: complete, to higher elevations of western states

Food: seeds, insects, will visit seed feeders

Compare: Similar to other rosy-finches, but the Gray-crowned has a black forehead, throat and chin. Much browner than Black Rosy-Finch (pg. 3), which is mostly black. The Brown-capped Rosy-Finch (pg. 103), the female Cassin's Finch (pg. 107) and female House Finch (pg. 83) lack the gray crown.

Stan's Notes: Found in the high alpine regions, nesting in steep cliff faces. Winter resident, breeding in Canada and Alaska. Almost always seen in small flocks, foraging on the ground near patches of snow. During breeding, both male and female develop an opening in the floor of mouth (buccal pouch), which is used for carrying a large supply of food, such as insects, to the young in the nest.

female

male pg. 267

CASSIN'S FINCH
Carpodacus cassinii

YEAR-ROUND
WINTER

Size: 6½" (16 cm)

Female: Brown-to-gray finch with fine black streaks on back and wings. Heavily streaked white chest and belly.

Male: light wash of crimson red, especially bright red crown, brown streaks on the back and wings, white belly

Juvenile: similar to female

Nest: cup; female builds; 1-2 broods per year

Eggs: 3-5; white without markings

Incubation: 12-14 days; female incubates

Fledging: 14-18 days; female and male feed young

Migration: partial migrator to non-migrator, will move around to find food

Food: seeds, insects, fruits, berries, will visit seed feeders

Compare: The female House Finch (pg. 83) is similar, but has a gray belly that is not as streaked. Lacks the characteristic gray head markings of the rosy-finches (pp. 3, 103 and 105).

Stan's Notes: Common high mountain finch of western Colorado, breeding in 8,000- to 11,000-foot (2,450 to 3,350 m) elevations starting in May or June. Usually forages for seeds on ground, but eats evergreen buds, and aspen and willow catkins. Colony nester, depending on the regional food source. The more food available, the larger the colony. Male sings a rapid warble, often imitating other birds such as jays, tanagers and grosbeaks. A cowbird host.

male pg. 29

female

non-breeding male

LARK BUNTING
Calamospiza melanocorys

MIGRATION
SUMMER

Size: 6½" (16 cm)

Female: Brown bird with heavily streaked chest and a white belly. White chin is flanked by two black lines. May have a central dark spot on the chest. Faint white eyebrows.

Male: black bird with a large broad head, white wing patches and large bluish-gray bill

Juvenile: similar to adult of the same sex

Nest: cup; female builds; 1-2 broods per year

Eggs: 4-6; pale blue with markings

Incubation: 11-13 days; female and male incubate

Fledging: 8-12 days; female and male feed young

Migration: complete, to southwestern states, Mexico

Food: insects, seeds

Compare: Appears similar to open country sparrows. Female Red-winged Blackbird (pg. 131) lacks the white belly and chin.

Stan's Notes: The state bird of Colorado. Thought to be the fourth most numerous bird in the state. Common in eastern Colorado in the dry plains and sagebrush regions. Has short rounded wings. Flies with shallow wing beats, with the male flashing its white wing patches. Male takes to the air to display to female, setting its wings in a V position and floating back, rocking like a butterfly, singing a most amazing song. Song is like the song of Old World larks, hence the common name. Will flock with hundreds, if not thousands, of other Lark Buntings in autumn for migration.

LARK SPARROW
Chondestes grammacus

Size: 6½" (16 cm)

Male: All-brown bird with unique rust red, white and black head pattern. White breast with a central black spot. Gray rump and white edges to gray tail, as seen in flight.

Female: same as male

Juvenile: similar to adult, but no rust red on head

Nest: cup, on the ground; female builds; 1 brood per year

Eggs: 3-6; pale white with brown markings

Incubation: 10-12 days; male and female incubate

Fledging: 10-12 days; female and male feed young

Migration: complete, to coastal Mexico and Central America

Food: seeds, insects

Compare: The White-throated Sparrow (pg. 113) and White-crowned Sparrow (pg. 115) both lack the Lark Sparrow's rust red pattern on the head and central spot on a white chest. Larger than the Chipping Sparrow (pg. 85), which has similar rusty color on head, but lacks Lark's white chest and central spot.

Stan's Notes: One of the larger sparrow species and one of the best songsters, also well known for its courtship strutting, chasing and lark-like flight pattern (rapid wing beats with tail spread). A bird of open fields, pastures and prairies, found almost anywhere there are no mountains. Very common during migration, when large flocks congregate. Uses nest for several years if first brood is successful.

white-striped

tan-striped

WHITE-THROATED SPARROW
Zonotrichia albicollis

Size: 6-7" (15-18 cm)

Male: A brown bird with gray tan chest and belly. Small yellow spot between the eyes (lore). Distinctive white or tan throat patch. White or tan stripes alternate with black stripes on crown. Color of the throat patch and crown stripes match.

Female: same as male

Juvenile: similar to adult, gray throat and eyebrows with heavily streaked chest

Nest: cup; female builds; 1 brood per year

Eggs: 4-6; varies between greenish, bluish and creamy white, with red brown markings

Incubation: 11-14 days; female incubates

Fledging: 10-12 days; female and male feed young

Migration: complete, to southern states and Mexico

Food: insects, seeds, fruit, visits ground feeders

Compare: White-crowned Sparrow (pg. 115) lacks yellow lore and white or tan throat patch. The Lark Sparrow (pg. 111) has a rust red pattern on the head and central black spot on a white chest.

Stan's Notes: There are two color variations (polymorphic) of the White-throated Sparrow: white-striped or tan-striped. Studies have indicated the white-striped adults tend to mate with the tan-striped birds. No indication why. Nests are built on the ground under small trees in bogs and coniferous forests.

juvenile

WHITE-CROWNED SPARROW
Zonotrichia leucophrys

YEAR-ROUND
MIGRATION
SUMMER
WINTER

Size: 6½-7½" (16-19 cm)

Male: A brown sparrow with a gray breast and a black-and-white striped crown. Small, thin pink bill.

Female: same as male

Juvenile: similar to adult, with brown stripes on the head instead of white

Nest: cup; female builds; 2 broods per year

Eggs: 3-5; varies between greenish, bluish and whitish, with red brown markings

Incubation: 11-14 days; female incubates

Fledging: 8-12 days; male and female feed young

Migration: complete, to southern states and Mexico

Food: insects, seeds, berries, visits ground feeders

Compare: The White-throated Sparrow (pg. 113) has a white or tan throat patch, and yellow spot between eyes and bill, with a blackish bill. The Lark Sparrow (pg. 111) has a rust red pattern on the head and central black spot on a white chest.

Stan's Notes: Usually seen in groups of up to 20 during the spring and autumn migrations. Males arrive before females and establish territories by singing from perches. Nests in mountainous central portion of the state. Nesting begins in May. Males take most of the responsibility of raising young while females start second broods. Only 9 to 12 days separate the broods. Feeds on the ground by scratching backward with both feet at the same time.

male pg. 63

female

BLUE GROSBEAK
Passerina caerulea

SUMMER

Size: 7" (18 cm)

Female: Overall brown with darker wings and tail. Two tan wing bars. Large gray-to-silver bill.

Male: blue bird with two chestnut-colored wing bars, a large gray-to-silver bill with black around base of bill

Juvenile: similar to female

Nest: cup; female builds; 1-2 broods per year

Eggs: 3-6; pale blue without markings

Incubation: 11-12 days; female incubates

Fledging: 9-10 days; female and male feed young

Migration: complete, to Central America, the Bahamas, Cuba and Mexico

Food: insects, seeds, will come to seed feeders

Compare: Female Lazuli Bunting (pg. 91) is similar, but has two narrow white wing bars and is a lighter color overall.

Stan's Notes: Blue Grosbeaks return to the state late, by mid-May. Most common in southeastern Colorado, but expanding northward with overall populations increasing over the past 30 to 40 years. A bird of semi-open habitats such as overgrown fields, riversides and woodland edges. Often seen twitching and spreading its tail. First-year males show only some blue, obtaining the full complement of blue feathers in the second winter. Will come to seed feeders.

HORNED LARK
Eremophila alpestris

YEAR-ROUND
SUMMER

Size: 7-8" (18-20 cm)

Male: A sleek tan-to-brown bird. Black necklace with a yellow chin and black bill. Two tiny "horns" on top of the head can be difficult to see. Black tail with white outer feathers noticeable in flight.

Female: same as male, only duller, "horns" are even less noticeable

Juvenile: lacks the black markings and yellow chin, doesn't form "horns" until second year

Nest: ground; female builds; 2-3 broods per year

Eggs: 3-4; gray with brown markings

Incubation: 11-12 days; female incubates

Fledging: 9-12 days; female and male feed young

Migration: partial migrator, Central and South America

Food: seeds, insects

Compare: Smaller than Meadowlark (pg. 309), which shares the black necklace and yellow chin. Look for the black marks in front of eyes.

Stan's Notes: The only true lark native to North America. A year-round resident, but also moves to find food (seasonal movement). Larks are birds of open ground. Common in rural areas, almost always seen in large flocks at country roads. Population increased over the past 100 years due to clearing land for farming. May have up to three broods per year because they get such an early start. Females perform a fluttering distraction display if nest is disturbed. Females can renest about seven days after brood fledges. The name "Lark" comes from the Middle English word *laverock*, or "a lark."

CEDAR WAXWING
Bombycilla cedrorum

SUMMER
WINTER

Size: 7½" (19 cm)

Male: Very sleek-looking gray-to-brown bird with pointed crest, light yellow belly and bandit-like black mask. Tip of tail is bright yellow and the tips of wings look as if they have been dipped in red wax.

Female: same as male

Juvenile: slightly smaller, overall gray, lacks red wing tips, black mask and sleek appearance, has a heavily streaked chest

Nest: cup; female and male build; 1 brood a year, occasionally 2

Eggs: 4-6; pale blue with brown markings

Incubation: 10-12 days; female incubates

Fledging: 14-18 days; female and male feed young

Migration: partial migrator, moves around to find food

Food: cedar cones, fruit, insects

Compare: Nearly identical to its larger, less common cousin, Bohemian Waxwing (not shown).

Stan's Notes: The name is derived from its red wax-like wing tips and preference for eating small blueberry-like cones of the cedar. Mostly seen in flocks, moving from area to area, looking for berries. Wanders in winter to find available food supplies. More often seen in winter only because naked branches reveal its presence. In the summer, before berries are abundant, it feeds on insects. Spends most of its time at the tops of tall trees. Listen for the very high-pitched whistling sounds that it constantly makes.

121

male pg. 5

female

BROWN-HEADED COWBIRD
Molothrus ater

SUMMER

Size: 7½" (19 cm)

Female: Dull brown bird with no obvious markings. Pointed, sharp gray bill.

Male: glossy black bird, chocolate brown head

Juvenile: similar to female, only dull gray color and a streaked chest

Nest: no nest; lays eggs in nests of other birds

Eggs: 5-7; white with brown markings

Incubation: 10-13 days; host bird incubates eggs

Fledging: 10-11 days; host birds feed young

Migration: complete, to southern states

Food: insects, seeds, will come to seed feeders

Compare: Female Red-winged Blackbird (pg. 131) is slightly larger, and has white eyebrows and a streaked chest. European Starling (pg. 7) has speckles and a shorter tail.

Stan's Notes: A member of the blackbird family. Of approximately 750 species of parasitic birds worldwide, this is the only parasitic bird in Colorado, laying all eggs in host birds' nests, leaving others to raise its young. Cowbirds are known to have laid eggs in nests of over 200 species of birds. Some birds reject cowbird eggs, but most raise them, even to the exclusion of their own young. Look for warblers and other birds feeding young birds twice their own size. At one time cowbirds followed bison to feed on the insects attracted to the animals.

COMMON POORWILL
Phalaenoptilus nuttallii

MIGRATION
SUMMER

Size: 7¾" (19.5 cm)

Male: A small all-brown bird with short tail and short rounded wings. White necklace and tip of tail.

Female: same as male

Juvenile: similar to adult

Nest: no nest; female scrapes a depression in the gravel; 1 brood per year

Eggs: 1-2; pale white with brown markings

Incubation: unknown days; incubation unknown

Fledging: unknown days; female and male feed the young

Migration: complete, to Central and South America

Food: insects

Compare: The Common Nighthawk (pg. 135) is very similar, but larger, with a long narrow tail and white band across each wing, as seen in flight.

Stan's Notes: Not much is known about this secretive species. It nests in open places below 8,000-foot (2,450 m) elevations. The excellent camouflage coloring and habit of not flushing off its nest or roosting make this bird hard to find and study. A nocturnal bird, usually only seen flying at dusk, flitting its wings more like a moth than a bird. Feeds on flying insects and drinks from the surface of water while in flight. Often easier to hear than to see at night. Gives a soft, low "poor-will" whistle, which accounts for the common name. Some that don't migrate have been found in a hibernation-like state (torpor).

winter

breeding

SPOTTED SANDPIPER
Actitis macularia

Size: 8" (20 cm)

Male: Olive brown back. Long bill and long dull yellow legs. White chest. A white line over the eyes. Breeding adult has black spots on chest. Winter adult lacks breast spots.

Female: same as male

Juvenile: similar to winter adult, with a darker bill

Nest: ground; female and male build; 2 broods per year

Eggs: 3-4; brownish with brown markings

Incubation: 20-24 days; male incubates

Fledging: 17-21 days; male feeds young

Migration: complete, to southern states, Mexico, and Central and South America

Food: aquatic insects

Compare: The Killdeer (pg. 143) has two black bands around neck. Look for Spotted Sandpiper to bob its tail up and down while standing. Look for the breeding Spotted Sandpiper's black spots extending from chest down to the abdomen.

Stan's Notes: One of the few sandpipers in Colorado. It is also one of the few shorebirds that will dive underwater if pursued. Able to fly straight up out of water. Flies with wings held in a cup-like arc, rarely lifting them above a horizontal plane. Constantly bobs its tail while standing and walks as if delicately balanced. Female mates with multiple males and lays eggs in up to five different nests. Male incubates and cares for young. In winter plumage, it lacks spots.

male pg. 263

female

BLACK-HEADED GROSBEAK
Pheucticus melanocephalus

MIGRATION
SUMMER

Size: 8" (20 cm)

Female: Appears like an overgrown sparrow. Overall brown with lighter-colored chest and belly, prominent white eyebrows and a large two-toned bill.

Male: burnt orange chest, neck and rump, black head, tail and wings with irregular-shaped white wing patches, large bill with upper bill darker than lower

Juvenile: similar to adult of the same sex

Nest: cup; female builds; 1 brood per year

Eggs: 3-4; pale green or bluish, brown markings

Incubation: 11-13 days; female and male incubate

Fledging: 11-13 days; female and male feed young

Migration: complete, to Central and South America

Food: insects, seeds, fruit

Compare: Female House Finch (pg. 83) is smaller, has more streaking on the chest and bill isn't as large. Look for female Grosbeak's unusual bicolored bill.

Stan's Notes: A cosmopolitan bird that nests in a wide variety of habitats, seeming to prefer the foothills in the western part of the state slightly more than other places. Breeds along two bands on the front range and western slopes from 5,000 to 8,000 feet (1,500 to 2,450 m). Both males and females sing, and aggressively defend their nests against intruders. Song is very similar to the American Robin's and Western Tanager's, making it difficult to tell them apart by song. Populations increasing in Colorado and across the U.S.

female

male pg. 11

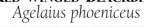

RED-WINGED BLACKBIRD
Agelaius phoeniceus

Size: 8½" (22 cm)

Female: Heavily streaked brown bird with a pointed brown bill and white eyebrows.

Male: jet black bird with red and yellow patches on upper wings, pointed black bill

Juvenile: same as female

Nest: cup; female builds; 2-3 broods per year

Eggs: 3-4; bluish green with brown markings

Incubation: 10-12 days; female incubates

Fledging: 11-14 days; female and male feed young

Migration: partial migrator to non-migrator, will move around the state to find food in winter

Food: seeds, insects, will come to seed feeders

Compare: Female Brewer's Blackbird (pg. 133) and female Yellow-headed Blackbird (pg. 139) are larger. Female Brown-headed Cowbird (pg. 123) is smaller. All three species lack white eyebrows and heavily streaked chest of the female Red-winged Blackbird.

Stan's Notes: One of the most widespread and numerous birds in Colorado. It is a sure sign of spring when Red-winged Blackbirds return to the marshes. Flocks of up to 100,000 birds have been reported. Males return before the females and defend territories by singing from the tops of surrounding vegetation. Will repeat call from top of cattail while showing off its red and yellow wing bars (epaulets). Nests are usually over shallow water in thick stands of cattails. They feed mostly on seeds in spring and fall, switching to insects during summer. Females choose mate.

male pg. 13

female

BREWER'S BLACKBIRD
Euphagus cyanocephalus

YEAR-ROUND
SUMMER

Size: 9" (22.5 cm)

Female: An overall grayish brown bird. Legs and bill nearly black. While most have dark eyes, some have bright white or pale yellow eyes.

Male: glossy black, shining green in direct light, head purplish, white or pale yellow eyes

Juvenile: similar to female

Nest: cup; female builds; 1-2 broods per year

Eggs: 4-6; gray with brown markings

Incubation: 12-14 days; female incubates

Fledging: 13-14 days; female and male feed young

Migration: complete, southwestern states and Mexico, partial to non-migrator in parts of Colorado

Food: insects, seeds, fruit

Compare: Larger in size and darker in color than the female Brown-headed Cowbird (pg. 123). Female Red-winged Blackbird (pg. 131) is similar in size, but has a heavily streaked chest and prominent white eyebrows.

Stan's Notes: A common blackbird of open areas such as farms, wet pastures, mountain meadows up to 10,000 feet (3,050 m) and even desert scrub. Usually nests in a shrub, small tree or directly on the ground. Prefers nesting in small colonies of up to 20 pairs. Doesn't get along with Common Grackles, often being driven out of nesting areas by expansion of the grackles. Will flock with other species such as Red-winged Blackbirds and cowbirds. A common cowbird host.

133

in flight

COMMON NIGHTHAWK
Chordeiles minor

SUMMER

Size: 9" (22.5 cm)

Male: A camouflaged brown and white bird with white chin. A distinctive white band across wings and the tail, seen only in flight.

Female: similar to male, but with tan chin, lacks the white tail band

Juvenile: similar to female

Nest: no nest; lays eggs on the ground, usually on rocks, or on rooftop; 1 brood per year

Eggs: 2; cream with lavender markings

Incubation: 19-20 days; female and male incubate

Fledging: 20-21 days; female and male feed young

Migration: complete, to South America

Food: insects caught in air

Compare: Common Poorwill (pg. 125) is similar, but smaller and has a shorter tail. Look for the obvious white wing band of Nighthawk in flight, and characteristic flap-flap-flap-glide flight pattern.

Stan's Notes: Usually only seen flying at dusk or after sunset, but not uncommon during day. Very noisy bird, repeating a "peenting" call during flight. Alternates slow wing beats with bursts of quick wing beats. Prolific insect eater. Prefers gravel rooftops for nesting. Male's distinctive springtime mating ritual is a steep diving flight terminated with a loud popping noise. One of the first birds to migrate each fall. Can be more common in cities than in country.

BURROWING OWL
Athene cunicularia

SUMMER

Size: 9½" (24 cm)

Male: A brown owl with bold white spots, white belly and very long legs. Yellow eyes.

Female: same as male

Juvenile: same as adult, but belly is brown

Nest: cavity, former mammal den, underground; 1 brood per year

Eggs: 6-11; white without markings

Incubation: 21-28 days; female incubates

Fledging: 25-28 days; female and male feed young

Migration: complete, to Mexico and Central America

Food: insects, mammals, lizards, birds

Compare: Smaller than Great Horned Owl (pg. 167) and lacking the feather tuft "horns." Spends most of the time on the ground, compared with the tree-loving Great Horned.

Stan's Notes: An owl of fields, open backyards, golf courses and airports. Nests in small family units or in small colonies. Takes over the underground dens of mammals, occasionally widening its den by kicking dirt backward. Lines den with cow pies, horse dung, grass and feathers. Some people have had success attracting these owls to their backyards by creating artificial dens. Often seen in the day, standing and sleeping around the den entrance. Male brings food to incubating female, often moving family to a new den when young are just a few weeks old.

137

male pg. 15

female

YELLOW-HEADED BLACKBIRD
Xanthocephalus xanthocephalus

SUMMER

Size:	9-11" (22.5-28 cm)
Female:	A large brown bird with a dull yellow head and chest. Slightly smaller than male.
Male:	black bird with a lemon-yellow head, chest and nape of neck, black mask and gray bill, white wing patches
Juvenile:	similar to female
Nest:	cup; female builds; 2 broods per year
Eggs:	3-5; greenish white with brown markings
Incubation:	11-13 days; female incubates
Fledging:	9-12 days; female feeds young
Migration:	complete, to southern states and Mexico
Food:	insects, seeds
Compare:	Larger than female Red-winged Blackbird (pg. 131), which has white eyebrows and streaked chest.

Stan's Notes: Usually heard before seen, Yellow-headed Blackbird has a low, hoarse, raspy or metallic call. Nests in deep water marshes unlike its cousin, the Red-winged Blackbird, which prefers shallow water. The male gives an impressive mating display, flying with head drooped and feet and tail pointing down while steadily beating its wings. The female incubates alone and feeds between three to five young. Young keep low and out of sight for up to three weeks before they start to fly. Migrates in flocks of up to 200 with grackles and cowbirds. Flocks consisting mainly of males return in late March and early April. Most colonies consist of between 20 to 100 nests.

BROWN THRASHER
Toxostoma rufum

MIGRATION
SUMMER

Size: 11" (28 cm)

Male: A rusty red bird with long tail and heavily streaked breast and belly. Two white wing bars. Long curved bill. Bright yellow eyes.

Female: same as male

Juvenile: same as adult, but eye color is grayish

Nest: cup; female and male build; 2 broods a year

Eggs: 4-5; pale blue with brown markings

Incubation: 11-14 days; female and male incubate

Fledging: 10-13 days; female and male feed young

Migration: complete, to southern states

Food: insects, fruit

Compare: Much larger than Sage Thrasher (pg. 205), which has a shorter tail and lacks any rusty red color. Slightly larger in size and similar in shape to the American Robin (pg. 211), but the Thrasher has a streaked chest, rusty color and bright yellow eyes.

Stan's Notes: A prodigious songster, often found in thick shrubs where it sings deliberate musical phrases, repeating each twice. The male has the largest documented song repertoire of all North American birds, with over 1,100 song types. Is often seen quickly flying or running in and out of thick or dense shrubs.

KILLDEER
Charadrius vociferus

YEAR-ROUND
SUMMER

Size: 11" (28 cm)

Male: An upland shorebird with two black bands around the neck like a necklace. A brown back and white belly. Bright reddish-orange rump, visible in flight.

Female: same as male

Juvenile: similar to adult, but only one neck band

Nest: ground; male builds; 2 broods per year

Eggs: 3-5; tan with brown markings

Incubation: 24-28 days; male and female incubate

Fledging: 25 days; male and female lead their young to food

Migration: complete, to southern states, Mexico and Central America

Food: insects

Compare: The Spotted Sandpiper (pg. 127) is found around water and lacks the two neck bands of the Killdeer.

Stan's Notes: The only shorebird with two black neck bands. It is known for its broken wing impression, which draws intruders away from nest. Once clear of the nest, the Killdeer takes flight. Nests are only a slight depression in a gravel area, often very difficult to see. Young look like yellow cotton balls on stilts. Able to follow parents and peck for insects soon after birth. Is technically classified as a shorebird, but doesn't live at the shore. Often found in vacant fields or along railroads. Has a very distinctive "kill-jer" call.

male

female

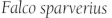

AMERICAN KESTREL
Falco sparverius

YEAR-ROUND
SUMMER

Size: 10-12" (25-30 cm)

Male: Rusty brown back and tail. A white breast with dark spots. Double black vertical lines on white face. Blue gray wings. Distinctive wide black band with a white edge on tip of rusty tail.

Female: similar to male, but slightly larger, has rusty brown wings and dark bands on tail

Juvenile: same as adult of the same sex

Nest: cavity; doesn't build a nest within; 1 brood per year

Eggs: 4-5; white with brown markings

Incubation: 29-31 days; male and female incubate

Fledging: 30-31 days; female and male feed young

Migration: non-migrator to partial migrator

Food: insects, small mammals and birds, reptiles

Compare: Similar to other falcons. Look for the two vertical black stripes on face of Kestrel. No other small bird of prey has rusty-colored back or tail.

Stan's Notes: Formerly called Sparrow Hawk due to its small size. Could be called Grasshopper Hawk because it eats many grasshoppers. Hovers near roads before diving for prey. Adapts quickly to a wooden nest box. Has pointed swept-back wings, seen in flight. Perches nearly upright. Kestrels are rare raptors in that males and females have quite different markings. Watch for them to pump their tails up and down after landing on perches.

red-shafted
male

yellow-shafted
female

red-shafted
female

yellow-shafted
male

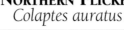

NORTHERN FLICKER
Colaptes auratus

YEAR-ROUND

Size:	12" (30 cm)
Male:	Brown and black woodpecker with a large white rump patch visible only when flying. Black necklace above speckled breast. Gray head with a brown cap. Red mustache.
Female:	same as male, but lacking red mustache
Juvenile:	same as adult of the same sex
Nest:	cavity; female and male excavate; 1 brood per year
Eggs:	5-8; white without markings
Incubation:	11-14 days; female and male incubate
Fledging:	25-28 days; female and male feed young
Migration:	non-migrator in Colorado
Food:	insects, especially ants and beetles
Compare:	Female Williamson's Sapsucker (pg. 37) has a finely barred back with a yellow belly and lacks Flicker's black spots on chest and belly.

Stan's Notes: The flicker is the only woodpecker to regularly feed on the ground, preferring ants and beetles. Produces antacid saliva to neutralize the acidic defense of ants. Male usually selects a nest site, taking up to 12 days to excavate. Some have been successful attracting flickers to nesting boxes stuffed with sawdust. Northern Flickers in western states flash reddish orange under the wings and tails when flying, while those in eastern states have golden yellow wing linings and tails. Both varieties undulate deeply during flight while giving a loud "wacka-wacka" call. Hybrids between western red-shafted and eastern yellow-shafted versions occur in the Great Plains, where their ranges overlap.

MOURNING DOVE
Zenaida macroura

Size: 12" (30 cm)

Male: Smooth fawn-colored dove with gray patch on the head. Iridescent pink, green around neck. A single black spot behind and below eyes. Black spots on wings and tail. Pointed wedge-shaped tail with white edges.

Female: similar to male, lacking iridescent pink and green neck feathers

Juvenile: spotted and streaked

Nest: platform; female and male build; 2 broods per year

Eggs: 2; white without markings

Incubation: 13-14 days; male and female incubate, the male during day, female at night

Fledging: 12-14 days; female and male feed young

Migration: complete to partial, to southern states, will move around to find food

Food: seeds, will come to seed feeders

Compare: Lacks the color combinations of Rock Dove (pg. 223). Similar to the Eurasian Collared-Dove (pg. 221), but lacks the black collar.

Stan's Notes: Name comes from its mournful cooing. Mates for life, roughly seven to ten years. A ground feeder, its head bobs as it walks. One of the few birds to drink without lifting head, same as Rock Dove. Parents feed the young a regurgitated liquid called crop-milk for the first few days of life. Flimsy platform nest of twigs often falls apart in a storm. Wind rushing through wing feathers in flight creates a characteristic whistling sound.

male pg. 21

female

GREAT-TAILED GRACKLE
Quiscalus mexicanus

SUMMER

Size:	15" (38 cm), female 18" (45 cm), male
Female:	An overall brown bird with gray-to-brown belly. Light brown eyes, eyebrows, throat, upper portion of chest.
Male:	all-black bird with iridescent purple sheen on head and back, exceptionally long tail, bright yellow eyes
Juvenile:	similar to female
Nest:	cup; female builds; 1-2 broods per year
Eggs:	3-5; greenish blue with brown markings
Incubation:	12-14 days; female incubates
Fledging:	21-23 days; female feeds young
Migration:	partial migrator to complete, moves around to find food
Food:	insects, fruit, seeds, comes to seed feeders
Compare:	Larger than the female Brewer's Blackbird (pg. 133), with a much lighter brown chest and distinct light brown eyebrows.

Stan's Notes: A bird that has expanded its range into Colorado recently, preferring to nest near water in an open habitat. Mainly in southern Colorado in elevations up to 8,000 feet (2,450 m), they are expanding northward and are expected to populate the entire state. Only a small percentage remains all winter. The rest move only far enough south to find food. Several females mate with one male. A colony nester, the males don't participate in nest building, incubation or the raising of young. Males rarely fight, but females will squabble over nest sites and materials.

male pg. 273

female

REDHEAD
Aythya americana

YEAR-ROUND
MIGRATION
SUMMER

Size: 19" (48 cm)

Female: Plain, soft brown duck with gray-to-white wing linings. Top of head is rounded. Two-toned bill, gray with a black tip.

Male: rich red head and neck with a black breast and tail, gray sides, smoky gray wings and back, tricolored bill with a light blue base, white ring and black tip

Juvenile: similar to female

Nest: cup; female builds; 1 brood per year

Eggs: 9-14; pale white without markings

Incubation: 24-28 days; female and male incubate

Fledging: 56-73 days; female shows the young what to eat

Migration: complete, to southern coastal states and Central America

Food: seeds, aquatic plants, insects

Compare: The female Northern Shoveler (pg. 157) is a lighter brown with an exceptionally large shovel-shaped bill.

Stan's Notes: A duck of permanent large bodies of water. Forages along the shoreline, feeding on seeds, aquatic plants and insects. Usually builds nest directly on surface of water, using large mats of vegetation. Female lays up to 75 percent of its eggs in the nests of other Redheads and several other duck species. Nests primarily in the Prairie Pothole region of the northern Great Plains. The overall populations seem to be increasing at approximately 2 to 3 percent each year.

female

male pg. 45

COMMON GOLDENEYE
Bucephala clangula

Size: 18½-20" (47-50 cm)

Female: A brown and gray duck with a large dark brown head, gray body, a white collar and bright golden eyes. Yellow-tipped dark bill.

Male: mostly white duck with black back, a large, puffy green head, with a large white spot in front of each bright golden eye, dark bill

Juvenile: same as female, but has a dark bill

Nest: cavity; female lines old woodpecker cavity; 1 brood per year

Eggs: 8-10; light green without markings

Incubation: 28-32 days; female incubates

Fledging: 56-59 days; female leads young to food

Migration: complete, to southern states

Food: aquatic plants, insects

Compare: Similar size as female Redhead (pg. 153), which is uniformly light brown, lacking the gray body of female Goldeneye. Look for female Goldeneye's dark brown head and white collar.

Stan's Notes: Known for their loud whistling, which is produced by their wings in flight. In late winter and early spring, males often attract females through elaborate displays, throwing their heads backward while uttering a single raspy note. Females will lay eggs in other goldeneye nests, resulting in some mothers incubating up to 30 eggs. Received its common name from its obvious bright golden eyes.

155

male pg. 251

female

NORTHERN SHOVELER
Anas clypeata

YEAR-ROUND
MIGRATION
SUMMER

Size: 20" (50 cm)

Female: Medium-sized brown duck speckled with black. Blue wing patch. An extraordinarily large spoon-shaped bill, almost always held pointed toward the water.

Male: same spoon-shaped bill, iridescent green head, rusty sides and white breast

Juvenile: same as female

Nest: ground; female builds; 1 brood per year

Eggs: 9-12; olive without markings

Incubation: 22-25 days; female incubates

Fledging: 30-60 days; female leads young to food

Migration: complete, southern states, Mexico, Central America, non-migrator in parts of Colorado

Food: aquatic insects, plants

Compare: Similar color as female Mallard (pg. 171), but Mallard lacks the Shoveler's large bill. Female Redhead (pg. 153) is overall lighter brown and has a dark gray bill with a black tip. Look for Shoveler's large spoon-shaped bill to help identify.

Stan's Notes: One of several species of shoveler, so called because of the peculiarly shaped bill. The Northern Shoveler is the only species of these ducks in North America. Seen in small flocks of five to ten, swimming low in water with large bills always pointed toward the water, as if they're too heavy to lift. Feeds primarily by filtering tiny plants and insects from the water's surface with bill.

female

male pg. 229

GADWALL
Anas strepera

Size: 20" (50 cm)

Female: Very similar to the female Mallard. Mottled brown with pronounced color change from dark brown body to light brown neck and head. Wing linings are bright white, seen in flight. Small white wing patch, seen when swimming. Gray bill with orange sides.

Male: plump gray duck with a brown head and distinctive black rump, white belly, bright white wing linings, small white wing patch, chestnut-tinged wings, gray bill

Juvenile: similar to female

Nest: ground; lined with fine grass, and down feathers plucked from mother's breast; 1 brood per year

Eggs: 8-11; white without markings

Incubation: 24-27 days; female incubates

Fledging: 48-56 days; young feed themselves

Migration: complete, to southern states, Mexico, non-migrator in parts of Colorado

Food: aquatic insects

Compare: The female Gadwall is very similar to female Mallard (pg. 171). Look for Gadwall's white wing patch and gray bill with orange sides.

Stan's Notes: A duck of shallow marshes with lots of vegetation. Most commonly seen during spring and fall migrations. Returns to Colorado in May, with breeding in June. Nests on land within 300 feet (100 m) of water. Establishes pair bond during winter.

male pg. 231

female

BLUE GROUSE
Dendragapus obscurus

YEAR-ROUND

Size: 20" (50 cm)

Female: A mottled brown chicken-like bird with a gray belly. Yellow patch of skin above eyes (comb) is not as obvious as in males. Tail is darker brown and squared off.

Male: dark gray bird with bright yellow-to-orange patch of skin above eyes (comb)

Juvenile: similar to female

Nest: ground; female builds; 1 brood per year

Eggs: 6-12; pale white with brown markings

Incubation: 24-26 days; female incubates

Fledging: 7-10 days; female feeds young

Migration: non-migrator to partial migrator, will move around to find food

Food: insects, seeds, fruit, buds, conifer needles

Compare: Smaller than female Ring-necked Pheasant (pg. 173) and lacking the long tail.

Stan's Notes: The most common grouse of the Rockies, seen from the foothills to the timberline. Usually on the ground, but also seen in trees feeding upon newly opened leaf buds in the spring. Often switches from an insect diet in summer to conifer needles (Douglas-Fir) in winter. The male engages in elaborate courtship displays that include fanning the tail, inflating its brightly colored neck sac and singing (calling). Male mates with several females. Young leave nest within 24 hours, following the mother around to feed. Very tame and will freeze when threatened, making it easy to get a close look.

soaring light morph

intermediate morph

light morph

dark morph

soaring dark morph

SWAINSON'S HAWK
Buteo swainsoni

SUMMER

Size: 21" (53 cm); up to 4½-foot wingspan

Male: Highly variable-plumaged hawk with three easily distinguishable color morphs. Light morph is brown with a white belly, a warm rusty breast and a white face. Intermediate has a dark breast, rusty belly and white at the base of the bill. Dark morph is nearly all dark brown with a rusty color low on belly.

Female: same as male

Juvenile: similar to adult

Nest: platform; female and male build; 1 brood per year

Eggs: 2-4; bluish or white, some brown markings

Incubation: 28-35 days; female and male incubate

Fledging: 28-30 days; female and male feed young

Migration: complete, to Central and South America

Food: small mammals, insects, snakes, birds

Compare: The Red-tailed Hawk (pg. 165) has a white chest with brown belly band. More slender than Red-tailed with longer, more pointed wings and longer tail.

Stan's Notes: Slender open country hawk that hunts mammals, insects, snakes and birds when soaring (kiting) or perching. Often flies with slightly upturned wings in a teetering, vulture-like flight. The light morph is the most common of the three color types, with intermediate and dark also common. Even minor nest disturbance can cause nest failure. Often gathers in large flocks to migrate.

soaring

RED-TAILED HAWK
Buteo jamaicensis

YEAR-ROUND
SUMMER

Size: 19-25" (48-63 cm); up to 4-foot wingspan

Male: Large hawk with amazing variety of colors from bird to bird, from chocolate brown to nearly all white. Often brown with a white breast and a distinctive brown belly band. Rust red tail usually only seen from above. Underside of wing is white with small dark patch on leading edge near shoulder.

Female: same as male, often larger

Juvenile: similar to adults, lacking the red tail, has a speckled chest

Nest: platform; male and female build; 1 brood per year

Eggs: 2-3; white, without markings or sometimes marked with brown

Incubation: 30-35 days; female and male incubate

Fledging: 45-46 days; male and female feed young

Migration: non-migrator to partial migrator, southern states

Food: mice, birds, snakes, insects

Compare: Swainson's Hawk (pg. 163) is slimmer with longer, more pointed wings.

Stan's Notes: A common hawk of open country and cities in the state, often seen perched on freeway light posts. Look for it circling above open fields, searching for prey. Their large stick nests are commonly seen along roads in large trees. Stick nests are lined with finer material such as evergreen needles. Will return to the same nest site each year. Doesn't develop red tail until second year.

165

GREAT HORNED OWL
Bubo virginianus

YEAR-ROUND

Size:	20-25" (50-63 cm)
Male:	A robust brown "horned" owl with bright yellow eyes and V-shaped white bib.
Female:	same as male, only slightly larger
Juvenile:	similar to adults
Nest:	no nest; takes over the nests of crows, Great Blue Herons and hawks, or will use partial cavities; 1 brood per year
Eggs:	2; white without markings
Incubation:	26-30 days; female incubates
Fledging:	30-35 days; male and female feed young
Migration:	non-migrator
Food:	small mammals, birds, snakes, insects
Compare:	Burrowing Owl (pg. 137) is smaller, has long legs and lacks the Great Horned Owl's feather tuft "horns."

Stan's Notes: The largest owl in the state. The earliest nesting bird in Colorado, it lays eggs in January and February. Has excellent hearing; able to hear a mouse moving under a foot of snow. "Ears" are actually tufts of feathers (horns) and have nothing to do with hearing. Not able to turn head all the way around. Wing feathers are ragged on the end, resulting in a silent flight. Eyelids close from the top down, like humans. Fearless, it is one of the few animals that will kill skunks and porcupines. Because of this, sometimes it is called Flying Tiger.

male pg. 233

female

NORTHERN HARRIER
Circus cyaneus

YEAR-ROUND
SUMMER

Size: 24" (60 cm)

Female: A slim, low-flying hawk. Dark brown back with brown-streaked breast and belly. Large white rump patch and narrow black bands across tail. Tips of wings black.

Male: silver gray with large white rump patch and white belly, faint narrow bands across tail, tips of wings black

Juvenile: similar to female, with an orange breast

Nest: platform; female and male build; 1 brood per year

Eggs: 4-8; bluish white without markings

Incubation: 31-32 days; female incubates

Fledging: 30-35 days; male and female feed young

Migration: partial to non-migrator, to southern states, Mexico and Central America

Food: mice, snakes

Compare: Slimmer than Red-tailed Hawk (pg. 165). Look for black bands on tail and a white rump patch.

Stan's Notes: One of the easiest hawks to identify. Harriers glide just above the ground, following the contours of the land while searching for prey. Wings are held just above the horizontal position, tilting back and forth in the wind, similar to Turkey Vultures. Was formerly called Marsh Hawk due to its habit of hunting over marshes. Nests on the ground. At all ages, the Northern Harrier has distinctive owl-like face disks.

male pg. 255

female

MALLARD
Anas platyrhynchos

YEAR-ROUND MIGRATION

Size: 27-28" (69-71 cm)

Female: All brown with orange and black bill. Small blue and white wing mark (speculum).

Male: large, bulbous green head, white necklace, rust brown or chestnut chest, combination of gray and white on sides, yellow bill, legs and feet

Juvenile: same as female, but with yellow bill

Nest: ground; female builds; 1 brood per year

Eggs: 7-10; greenish to whitish, unmarked

Incubation: 26-30 days; female incubates

Fledging: 42-52 days; female leads young to food

Migration: partial migrator to non-migrator

Food: seeds, plants, aquatic insects, will come to ground feeders offering corn

Compare: Female Gadwall (pg. 159) has a gray bill with orange sides, unlike female Mallard's orange and black bill. The female Northern Shoveler (pg. 157) is smaller, with a large spoon-shaped bill.

Stan's Notes: A familiar duck of lakes and ponds. Will return to place of birth. The name "Mallard" comes from the Latin *masculus*, meaning "male," referring to the habit of males not taking part in raising ducklings. Both male and female have white tails and white underwings. Black central tail feathers of male curl upward.

male

female

RING-NECKED PHEASANT
Phasianus colchicus

YEAR-ROUND

Size: 30-36" (76-90 cm), male, including tail
21-25" (53-63 cm), female, including tail

Male: Golden brown body with a long tail. White ring around neck with purple, green, blue and red head.

Female: smaller, less flamboyant all-brown bird with a long tail

Juvenile: similar to female, with shorter tail

Nest: ground; female builds; 1 brood per year

Eggs: 8-10; olive brown without markings

Incubation: 23-25 days; female incubates

Fledging: 11-12 days; female leads young to food

Migration: non-migrator

Food: insects, seeds, fruit, visits ground feeders

Compare: The male and female Blue Grouse (pp. 231 and 161, respectively) are smaller and lack a long tail. The male Ring-necked Pheasant is brightly colored.

Stan's Notes: Introduced from China in the late 1800s. Common now across the U.S. Like many other game birds, their numbers vary greatly, making them common some years and scarce others. The name "Ring-necked" refers to the thin white ring around the male's neck. The name "Pheasant" comes from the Greek word *phaisianos*, meaning "a bird of the River Phasis," which is now known as the River Rioni, located in Europe. Listen for the male's cackling call to attract females.

soaring

juvenile

GOLDEN EAGLE
Aquila chrysaetos

YEAR-ROUND
WINTER

Size: 30-40" (76-102 cm); up to 7-foot wingspan

Male: Uniform dark brown with golden head and nape of neck. Yellow around the base of bill and yellow feet.

Female: same as male

Juvenile: similar to adult, but has white wrist patches and white base of tail

Nest: platform, on cliff; female and male build; 1 brood per year

Eggs: 2; white with brown markings

Incubation: 43-45 days; female and male incubate

Fledging: 66-75 days; female and male feed young

Migration: partial migrator to non-migrator

Food: mammals, birds, reptiles, insects

Compare: Similar to Bald Eagle (pg. 55), lacking the white head and tail. Juvenile Golden Eagle, with its white wrist marks and white base of tail, is often confused with the juvenile Bald Eagle.

Stan's Notes: Large and powerful bird of prey that has no trouble taking larger prey such as jack rabbits. Hunts by perching or soaring and watching for movement. Inhabits mountainous terrain, requiring large territories to provide large supply of food. Thought to mate for life, renewing pair bond late in winter with spectacular high-flying courtship displays. Usually nests on cliff faces, rarely in trees. Uses well-established nest that has been used for generations. Not uncommon for it to add things to nest such as antlers, bones and barbed wire.

WILD TURKEY
Meleagris gallopavo

Size: 36-48" (90-120 cm)

Male: Large, plump brown and bronze bird with striking blue and red bare head. Fan tail and long, straight black beard in center of chest. Spurs on legs.

Female: thinner and less striking than male, usually lacking breast beard

Juvenile: same as adult of the same sex

Nest: ground; female builds; 1 brood per year

Eggs: 10-12; buff white with dull brown markings

Incubation: 27-28 days; female incubates

Fledging: 6-10 days; female leads young to food

Migration: non-migrator

Food: insects, seeds, fruit

Compare: This bird is quite distinctive and unlikely to be confused with others.

Stan's Notes: The largest game bird in the state, and the bird from which the domestic turkey was bred. Almost became our national bird, but lost by one vote to the Bald Eagle. Nearly eliminated from Colorado by the turn of the twentieth century due to market hunting and loss of habitat. Restoration efforts began in the 1930s and continue today. Strong fliers, they can approach 60 miles (97 km) per hour. Able to fly straight up, then away. Eyesight is three times better than humans. Hearing is also excellent; can hear competing males up to a mile away. Males hold "harems" of up to 20 females. Males are known as toms, females are hens and young are called poults. At night, they roost in trees.

RUBY-CROWNED KINGLET
Regulus calendula

MIGRATION
SUMMER
WINTER

Size: 4" (10 cm)

Male: Small, teardrop-shaped green-to-gray bird. Two white wing bars. Hidden ruby-colored crown. White eye ring.

Female: same as male, but lacks ruby crown

Juvenile: same as female

Nest: pendulous; female builds; 1 brood per year

Eggs: 4-5; white with brown markings

Incubation: 11-12 days; female incubates

Fledging: 11-12 days; female and male feed young

Migration: complete, to southern states, Mexico and Central America

Food: insects, berries

Compare: The female American Goldfinch (pg. 289) is larger, but shares the same olive color and unmarked breast. Look for the white eye ring of Ruby-crowned Kinglet.

Stan's Notes: One of the smaller birds in the state, it takes a quick eye to see the male's ruby crown. Most commonly seen during the spring and autumn migrations, look for it flitting around thick shrubs low to the ground. Builds an unusual pendulous (sac-like) nest, intricately woven and decorated on the outside with colored lichens and mosses stuck together with spider webs. The nest is suspended from a branch overlapped by leaves, usually hung high in a mature tree. The name "Kinglet" comes from the Anglo-Saxon *cyning*, or "king," referring to its ruby crown, and the diminutive suffix "let," meaning "small."

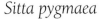

PYGMY NUTHATCH
Sitta pygmaea

YEAR-ROUND

Size: 4¼" (10.5 cm)

Male: Tiny gray-blue black bird with gray-brown crown. Creamy chest with a lighter chin. A relatively short tail, large head and long bill.

Female: same as male

Juvenile: same as adult

Nest: cavity; the female and male build; 1 brood per year

Eggs: 4-8; white with brown markings

Incubation: 14-16 days; female incubates

Fledging: 20-22 days; female and male feed young

Migration: non-migrator

Food: insects, berries, seeds, will visit seed feeders

Compare: Smaller than the Red-breasted Nuthatch (pg. 183) and the White-breasted Nuthatch (pg. 191). The Red-breasted has a rusty red chest, compared with the creamy breast of the Pygmy. White-breasted has a distinctive black cap and a white chest.

Stan's Notes: A common bird of Ponderosa Pine forest along the front range. Unlike White-breasted Nuthatches, Pygmy Nuthatches need mature ponderosas with old or decaying wood. Usually drills its own nest cavity. While it doesn't migrate, it forms winter flocks with other birds, such as chickadees and creepers, moving around in search of food. Usually feeds in the crown of a tree or at ends of twigs and branches, where it searches for insects and seeds, unlike the White-breasted and Red-breasted Nuthatches, which usually search trunks of trees for food.

RED-BREASTED NUTHATCH
Sitta canadensis

YEAR-ROUND
MIGRATION
WINTER

Size: 4½" (11 cm)

Male: A small gray-backed bird with a black cap and a prominent eye line. A rust red breast and belly.

Female: gray cap, pale undersides

Juvenile: same as female

Nest: cavity; female builds; 1 brood per year

Eggs: 5-6; white with red brown markings

Incubation: 11-12 days; female incubates

Fledging: 14-20 days; female and male feed young

Migration: non-migrator to irruptive, moves around in search of food

Food: insects, seeds, visits seed and suet feeders

Compare: Slightly larger than the Pygmy Nuthatch (pg. 181) and smaller than White-breasted Nuthatch (pg. 191), neither of which has the rich red breast of the Red-breasted.

Stan's Notes: Red-breasted Nuthatch behaves like White-breasted and Pygmy Nuthatches, climbing down trunks of trees headfirst. Similar to chickadees, visits seed feeders, quickly grabbing a seed and flying off to crack it open. Will wedge a seed into a crevice and pound it open with several sharp blows. The name "Nuthatch" comes from the Middle English moniker *nuthak*, referring to the bird's habit of wedging a seed into a crevice and hacking it open. Look for it in mature conifers, frequently extracting seeds from cones. Doesn't excavate a cavity as the chickadee might; rather, it takes over a former woodpecker or chickadee cavity.

BLACK-CAPPED CHICKADEE
Poecile atricapilla

YEAR-ROUND
SUMMER

Size: 5" (13 cm)

Male: Familiar gray bird with black cap and throat patch. White chest. Tan belly. Small white wing marks.

Female: same as male

Juvenile: same as adult

Nest: cavity; female and male build or excavate; 1 brood per year

Eggs: 5-7; white with fine brown markings

Incubation: 11-13 days; female and male incubate

Fledging: 14-18 days; female and male feed young

Migration: non-migrator to partial migrator

Food: insects, seeds, fruit, will visit seed and suet feeders

Compare: Mountain Chickadee (pg. 187) is similar, but has white eyebrows.

Stan's Notes: A common backyard bird that can be attracted with a simple nest box. Makes nest mostly with green moss and lines it with animal fur. Usually the first bird to find a new bird feeder. Can be easily tamed and hand fed. Needs to feed every day during the winter; consequently seen foraging for food during even the worst winter storms. Can have different calls in various regions.

MOUNTAIN CHICKADEE
Poecile gambeli

YEAR-ROUND
WINTER

Size: 5½" (14 cm)

Male: Overall gray with a black cap, chin and line through the eyes. White eyebrows.

Female: same as male

Juvenile: similar to adult

Nest: cavity, old woodpecker hole or excavates its own; female and male build; 1-2 broods per year

Eggs: 5-8; white without markings

Incubation: 11-14 days; female and male incubate

Fledging: 18-21 days; female and male feed young

Migration: partial migrator

Food: seeds, insects, visits seed and suet feeders

Compare: The Black-capped Chickadee (pg. 185) is similar, but lacks the white eyebrows of the Mountain Chickadee.

Stan's Notes: Thought to be one of the top ten most abundant birds in Colorado. More common in western Colorado's conifer forest, preferring old growth spruce, fir and Lodgepole Pine forest. Feeds heavily on conifer seeds, and insects. Usually doesn't mingle with Black-capped Chickadees, but does flock with other birds in winter. Moves to lower elevations during winter, returning to high elevations for nesting. Nests in a cavity that it excavates or uses an old woodpecker hole. Will use a nest box. Occasionally uses same nest site year after year. Lines its nest with moss, hair and feathers. Female won't leave nest if disturbed, but will hiss and flutter wings.

female pg. 89

male

gray-headed

Oregon male

DARK-EYED JUNCO
Junco hyemalis

YEAR-ROUND
WINTER

Size: 5½" (14 cm)

Male: A round, dark-eyed bird with slate-gray-to-charcoal chest, head and back. White belly. Pink bill. Since the outermost tail feathers are white, tail appears as a white V in flight.

Female: same as male, only tan-to-brown color

Juvenile: similar to female, but has a streaked breast and head

Nest: cup; female and male build; 2 broods a year

Eggs: 3-5; white with reddish brown markings

Incubation: 12-13 days; female incubates

Fledging: 10-13 days; male and female feed young

Migration: partial migrator to complete, across the U.S.

Food: seeds, insects, will come to seed feeders

Compare: Rarely confused with any other bird. Large flocks come to feed under bird feeders.

Stan's Notes: Several junco species have now been combined into one, simply called Dark-eyed Junco (see inset photos). Estimates of over 2 million juncos found in Colorado, making it one of the most numerous breeding birds in the state. Common year-round bird of Colorado, spending winters in foothills and plains after snowmelt, returning to higher elevations for nesting. Nests in a wide variety of wooded habitats in April and May. Usually seen on the ground in small flocks. It adheres to a rigid social hierarchy, with dominant birds chasing the less dominant birds. Look for its white outer tail feathers flashing in flight. Most comfortable on the ground, juncos will "double-scratch" with both feet to expose seeds and insects. Consumes many weed seeds.

WHITE-BREASTED NUTHATCH
Sitta carolinensis

YEAR-ROUND
SUMMER
WINTER

Size: 5-6" (13-15 cm)

Male: Slate gray with a white face and belly, and black cap and nape. Long thin bill, slightly upturned. Chestnut undertail.

Female: similar to male, gray cap and nape

Juvenile: similar to female

Nest: cavity; the female and male build; 1 brood per year

Eggs: 5-7; white with brown markings

Incubation: 11-12 days; female incubates

Fledging: 13-14 days; female and male feed young

Migration: non-migrator to partial migrator

Food: insects, seeds, visits seed and suet feeders

Compare: Red-breasted Nuthatch (pg. 183) is smaller, with a rusty belly and distinctive black eye line. Pygmy Nuthatch (pg. 181) is smaller and lacks the White-breasted's black cap.

Stan's Notes: The nuthatch's habit of hopping headfirst down tree trunks helps it see insects and insect eggs that birds climbing up the trunk might miss. Incredible climbing agility comes from an extra-long hind toe claw or nail, nearly twice the size of the front toe claws. The name "Nuthatch" comes from the Middle English moniker *nuthak*, referring to the bird's habit of wedging a seed into a crevice and hacking it open. Often seen in mixed flocks of Brown Creepers, chickadees and Downy Woodpeckers. Mated pairs stay together all year, defending small territories. Listen for its characteristic springtime call, "whi-whi-whi-whi," given in February and March. One of 17 worldwide nuthatch species.

male

female

YELLOW-RUMPED WARBLER
Dendroica coronata

MIGRATION
SUMMER

Size: 5-6" (13-15 cm)

Male: Slate gray bird with black mask and breast. Yellow patch on the head, flanks and rump. White chin and belly. Two white wing bars.

Female: similar to male, duller color, mostly brown and white with matching yellow patches

Juvenile: similar to female

Nest: cup; female builds; 2 broods per year

Eggs: 4-5; white with brown markings

Incubation: 12-13 days; female incubates

Fledging: 10-12 days; female and male feed young

Migration: complete, to southern states, Mexico and Central America

Food: insects, berries, rarely comes to suet feeders

Compare: The Common Yellowthroat (pg. 291) has a yellow breast, unlike the Yellow-rumped's patches of yellow. The male Yellow Warbler (pg. 295) is all yellow with orange streaks on breast. Male Wilson's Warbler (pg. 287) has a characteristic black crown. Look for a combination of yellow patches on the head, flanks and rump.

Stan's Notes: The most common warbler in Colorado, nesting in conifer and aspen forests on mountains between 7,000 and 12,000 feet (2,150 to 3,650 m). Was formerly called Audubon's Warbler. Sometimes called Butter-butts due to the yellow patch on rump. Males molt to a dull color similar to females each winter, retaining yellow patches. Familiar call is a robust "chip."

WESTERN WOOD-PEWEE
Contopus sordidulus

MIGRATION
SUMMER

Size: 6¼" (15.5 cm)

Male: An overall gray bird with darker wings and tail. Two narrow gray wing bars. Dull white throat with pale yellow or white belly. Black upper bill, dull orange lower.

Female: same as male

Juvenile: similar to adult, lacking the two-toned bill

Nest: cup; female builds; 1 brood per year

Eggs: 2-4; pale white with brown markings

Incubation: 12-14 days; female incubates

Fledging: 14-18 days; female and male feed young

Migration: complete, to Central and South America

Food: insects

Compare: Olive-sided Flycatcher (pg. 199) is larger, has a white patch on the sides of rump and lacks Wood-Pewee's distinct wing bars and darker wings.

Stan's Notes: A widespread bird in Colorado, most commonly found in aspen forest and near water. Requires trees with dead tops or branches from which to sing and hunt for flying insects, which compose nearly all of the diet. Often returns to the same perch after each foray. Nests throughout western North America from Alaska to Mexico. Overall populations are decreasing about 1 percent each year. Common name comes from a nasal whistle, "pee-wee."

SAY'S PHOEBE
Sayornis saya

Size: 7½" (19 cm)

Male: Overall dark gray, darkest on head, tail and wings. Belly and undertail tawny. Black bill.

Female: same as male

Juvenile: similar to adult, but is browner overall with two tawny wing bars and yellow lower bill

Nest: cup; female builds; 1-2 broods per year

Eggs: 3-6; pale white with brown markings

Incubation: 12-14 days; female incubates

Fledging: 14-16 days; female and male feed young

Migration: complete, to Central and South America

Food: insects, berries

Compare: The Olive-sided Flycatcher (pg. 199) is the same size, but has a white patch on sides of rump and lacks the Phoebe's tawny belly. Western Wood-Pewee (pg. 195) is smaller and also lacks the tawny belly.

Stan's Notes: A widespread bird in Colorado below 9,000-foot (2,750 m) elevations. Nests in cliff crevices, abandoned buildings, bridges and other vertical structures. Catches flying insects in flight or by hovering and dropping to the ground. Nearly all-insect diet. Often uses the same nest several times in a season, returning the following year to the same nest.

OLIVE-SIDED FLYCATCHER
Contopus cooperi

MIGRATION
SUMMER

Size: 7½" (19 cm)

Male: An all-dark-gray flycatcher with dull white chin, breast and belly. Characteristic white patch on sides of rump, seen when the bird relaxes its wings while perching.

Female: same as male

Juvenile: similar to adult

Nest: cup; female builds; 1 brood per year

Eggs: 3-4; white with brown markings

Incubation: 12-14 days; female incubates

Fledging: 21-23 days; female and male feed young

Migration: complete, to South America

Food: insects

Compare: Western Wood-Pewee (pg. 195) is smaller, has darker wings and lacks the white patch on the sides of Olive-sided's rump.

Stan's Notes: Solitary bird of mountainous conifer forest in western Colorado. Often seen perched at the tops of dead tree snags, singing or looking (hawking) for flying insects. Once it has spotted an insect, it flies off its perch to snatch it up, then returns to the perch to eat. Seems to prefer bees, flies, grasshoppers and small dragonflies. Populations decreasing yearly in Colorado.

AMERICAN DIPPER
Cinclus mexicanus

YEAR-ROUND

Size: 7½" (19 cm)

Male: Dark gray to black overall, slightly lighter-colored head. Short upturned tail, and dark eyes and bill.

Female: same as male

Juvenile: similar to adult, only paler with white eyelids that are most noticeable when blinking

Nest: pendulous, covered nest with the entrance near the bottom, on cliff, behind waterfall; female builds; 1-2 broods per year

Eggs: 3-5; white without markings

Incubation: 13-17 days; female incubates

Fledging: 18-25 days; female and male feed young

Migration: non-migrator, seeks moving open water

Food: aquatic insects, small fish, crustaceans

Compare: Similar shape as American Robin (pg. 211), but lacks a red breast. The only songbird in Colorado that dives into fast-moving water.

Stan's Notes: A common bird of fast, usually noisy streams that provide some kind of protected shelf on which to construct nest. Some have had success attracting with man-made ledges. Plunges headfirst into fast-moving water, looking for just about any aquatic insect, propelling itself underwater with wings. Often seen emerging with a large insect, which it smashes against rock before eating. Depending on snowmelt, nesting usually starts in March or April. American Dippers in elevations below 6,000 feet (1,850 m) often nest for a second time each season.

EASTERN KINGBIRD
Tyrannus tyrannus

SUMMER

Size: 8" (20 cm)

Male: Mostly black gray bird with white belly and chin. Black head and tail with a distinctive white band across the end of the tail. Has a concealed red crown that is rarely seen.

Female: same as male

Juvenile: same as adult

Nest: cup; male and female build; 1 brood a year

Eggs: 3-4; white with brown markings

Incubation: 16-18 days; female incubates

Fledging: 16-18 days; female and male feed young

Migration: complete, to Mexico, Central America and South America

Food: insects, fruit

Compare: Rarely confused with other birds. Lacks any yellow of the Western Kingbird (pg. 307). Medium-sized bird, smaller than American Robin (pg. 211). Look for the white band along the end of the tail to identify.

Stan's Notes: A common bird of open fields and prairies. Acting unafraid of other birds and chasing the larger ones, it is perceived as having an attitude. Bold behavior gave rise to its common name, King. Perches on tall branches, watching for insects. After flying out to catch them, it returns to the same perch, a technique called hawking. Male and female return to mating ground and defend a territory together.

SAGE THRASHER
Oreoscoptes montanus

MIGRATION
SUMMER

Size: 8½" (22 cm)

Male: Light gray overall with a heavily streaked white chest. Distinctive white chin. Yellow orange eyes. Darker gray tail with white tip.

Female: same as male

Juvenile: duller version of adult

Nest: cup; the female and male build; 1-2 broods per year

Eggs: 3-5; blue with brown markings

Incubation: 13-17 days; female and male incubate

Fledging: 11-14 days; female and male feed young

Migration: complete, to Mexico and Central America

Food: insects, fruit

Compare: Smaller than the Brown Thrasher (pg. 141), Sage Thrasher has a shorter tail and is not rusty red.

Stan's Notes: More common in the sagebrush regions of the state. Sagebrush regions are well known for the lack of bird life. Males are often seen and heard as they sing from the tops of shrubs. Will construct a large and bulky nest at the base of or beneath dense cover in an attempt to keep the nest shaded. Sometimes constructs a twig platform over nest if existing cover doesn't provide enough shade. Returns in April. Nesting in May. Populations increasing in Colorado over the past few decades.

LOGGERHEAD SHRIKE
Lanius ludovicianus

SUMMER

Size: 9" (22.5 cm)

Male: A gray head and back with black wings and mask across the eyes. A white chin, breast and belly. Black tail, legs and feet. Black bill with hooked tip. White wing patches, seen in flight.

Female: same as male

Juvenile: dull version of adult

Nest: cup; the male and female build; 1-2 broods per year

Eggs: 4-7; off-white with dark markings

Incubation: 16-17 days; female incubates

Fledging: 17-21 days; female and male feed young

Migration: complete, to southern states and Mexico

Food: insects, lizards, small mammals, frogs

Compare: The Northern Mockingbird (pg. 213) has a similar color pattern, but lacks the black mask of the Loggerhead. Shrike is stockier than the Mockingbird and perches in more open places.

Stan's Notes: The Loggerhead is a songbird that acts like a bird of prey. Known for skewering prey on barbed wire fences, thorns and other sharp objects to store or hold still while tearing apart to eat, hence its other name, Butcher Bird. Feet are too weak to hold prey while eating. Most common in the eastern half of the state, where it depends on short grass prairie habitat. On the decline overall due to pesticides killing its major food source–grasshoppers.

male pg. 271

female

PINE GROSBEAK
Pinicola enucleator

YEAR-ROUND
WINTER

Size: 9" (22.5 cm)

Female: A plump gray winter finch with a long dark tail. Dark wings with two white wing bars. Head and rump tinged dull yellow. Short, stubby, pointed dark bill.

Male: overall rosy red and gray

Juvenile: female is similar to adult female, male has a touch of red on head and rump

Nest: cup; female builds; 1 brood per year

Eggs: 4-5; bluish green without markings

Incubation: 13-15 days; female incubates

Fledging: 13-20 days; female and male feed young

Migration: non-migrator to irruptive, moves around to find food

Food: seeds, fruit, insects, will come to feeders

Compare: Much larger than the female House Finch (pg. 83). Female Red Crossbill (pg. 297) is smaller, with crossed bill and no wing bars.

Stan's Notes: Very tame and approachable bird. Often seen along roads or on the ground, eating tiny grains of sand and dirt to aid in digestion. A seed eater that favors conifer woods, rarely moving out of the conifer regions during summer. During the winter, it will move down from higher regions to the foothills in search of food. Often seen bathing in fluffy snow. Flies with a typical finch-like undulating pattern while calling a soft whistle. During breeding season, both male and female develop a pouch in the bottom of the mouth (buccal pouch) to transport seeds to young.

male

female

AMERICAN ROBIN
Turdus migratorius

Size: 9-11" (22.5-28 cm)

Male: A familiar gray bird with a rusty red breast, and nearly black head and tail. White chin with black streaks. White eye ring.

Female: similar to male, but with a gray head and a duller breast

Juvenile: similar to female, but has a speckled breast and brown back

Nest: cup; female builds with help from the male; 2-3 broods per year

Eggs: 4-7; pale blue without markings

Incubation: 12-14 days; female incubates

Fledging: 14-16 days; female and male feed young

Migration: complete, southern states, Mexico, Central America, small percentage non-migrator

Food: insects, fruit, berries, worms

Compare: Familiar bird to all.

Stan's Notes: Although complete migrators, they can be seen year-round in some parts of the state. Why it is that some don't migrate is not known. Can be heard singing all night long in spring. Most people don't realize how easy it is to tell the difference between the male and female robin. Look for the male's dark, nearly black head and brick-red chest, compared with the female's gray head and dull red chest. Robins are not listening for worms when they cock their heads to one side or the other. They are looking with eyes that are placed far back on the sides of their heads. A very territorial bird. Often seen fighting its own reflection in windows.

displaying

NORTHERN MOCKINGBIRD
Mimus polyglottos

SUMMER

Size: 10" (25 cm)

Male: Silvery gray head and back with light gray chest and belly. White wing patches, seen in flight or during display. Tail mostly black with white outer tail feathers. Black bill.

Female: same as male

Juvenile: overall dull gray, a heavily streaked breast, gray bill

Nest: cup; female and male build; 2 broods per year, sometimes more

Eggs: 3-5; blue green with brown markings

Incubation: 12-13 days; female incubates

Fledging: 11-13 days; female and male feed young

Migration: complete, to southern states

Food: insects, fruit

Compare: Loggerhead Shrike (pg. 207) has a similar color pattern, but is stockier, has a black mask and perches in more open places. Look for Mockingbird to spread its wings, flash its white wing patches and wag its tail from side to side.

Stan's Notes: Very animated, male and female perform elaborate mating dances by facing each other, heads and tails erect. They run toward each other, flashing white wing patches, and then retreat to nearby cover. Thought to also flash wing patches to scare up insects when hunting. Known to imitate other birds (vocal mimicry), hence its common name. Young males often sing at night.

GRAY JAY
Perisoreus canadensis

Size: 11½" (29 cm)

Male: Large gray bird with a gray patch on back of head. White patch on forehead. White nape and breast. Short black bill. Dark eyes.

Female: same as male

Juvenile: sooty gray with a faint white whisker mark

Nest: cup; male and female build; 1 brood a year

Eggs: 3-4; gray white, finely marked to unmarked

Incubation: 16-18 days; female incubates

Fledging: 14-15 days; male and female feed young

Migration: non-migrator

Food: insects, seeds, fruit, nuts, visits seed feeders

Compare: Similar in size to Steller's Jay (pg. 71) and Blue Jay (pg. 73), but lacks any blue and a crest. The Clark's Nutcracker (pg. 217) is slightly larger and has black wings. Black-billed Magpie (pg. 47) is nearly twice the size of Gray Jay, has a much longer tail and lacks the mostly white head.

Stan's Notes: A bird of conifer woods in elevations of 8,500 feet (2,600 m) and higher. Called Camp Robber because it rummages through camps looking for scraps of food. Also called Whisky Jack or Canada Jay. Easily tamed, it will fly to your hand if offered raisins or nuts. Will eat just about anything. Will also store extra food for winter, balling it together in a sticky mass, placing it on a tree limb, often concealing it with lichen or bark. Travels in small family units of three to five, making good companions for high altitude hikers or climbers. Reminds some people of an overgrown chickadee.

CLARK'S NUTCRACKER
Nucifraga columbiana

YEAR-ROUND

Size: 12" (30 cm)

Male: All-gray bird with black wings and narrow black band down the center of tail. Small white patches on long wings, seen in flight. A relatively short tail with white undertail.

Female: same as male

Juvenile: same as adult

Nest: cup; female and male build; 1 brood a year

Eggs: 2-5; pale green with brown markings

Incubation: 16-18 days; female and male incubate

Fledging: 18-20 days; female and male feed young

Migration: non-migrator

Food: seeds, insects, berries, eggs, mammals

Compare: Slightly larger than the Gray Jay (pg. 215), which lacks the Nutcracker's black wings. The Steller's Jay (pg. 71) is dark blue with a black crest.

Stan's Notes: A high country bird found in conifer forest in the western half of the state. While it has a varied diet, it relies heavily on piñon seeds, often caching large amounts to consume later or feed young. Has a large pouch in throat (sublingual pouch), which it uses to transport seeds. Studies show the birds can carry up to 100 seeds at a time. Nests early in the year while snow still covers the ground, relying on stored foods.

soaring

SHARP-SHINNED HAWK
Accipiter striatus

YEAR-ROUND
MIGRATION
SUMMER
WINTER

Size: 10-14" (25-36 cm)

Male: Small woodland hawk with gray back and head, and rusty red breast. Long tail with several dark tail bands, widest band at end of squared-off tail. Red eyes.

Female: same as male, only larger

Juvenile: same size as adults, with a brown back and heavily streaked breast, yellow eyes

Nest: platform; female builds; 1 brood per year

Eggs: 4-5; white with brown markings

Incubation: 32-35 days; female incubates

Fledging: 24-27 days; female and male feed young

Migration: complete, to southern states, Mexico and Central America

Food: birds, small mammals

Compare: Nearly identical to Cooper's Hawk (pg. 227), only smaller. Look for squared end of tail on the Sharp-shinned, compared with the round end of Cooper's.

Stan's Notes: A common hawk of backyards and woodland, often seen swooping in on birds visiting feeders. Short rounded wings and long tail allow this hawk to navigate through thick stands of trees in pursuit of prey. Common name comes from the sharp keel on the leading edge of its "shin," although it is actually below rather than above the bird's ankle on the tarsus bone of foot. The tarsus in most birds is round. In flight, head doesn't protrude as far as the head of the Cooper's Hawk.

EURASIAN COLLARED-DOVE
Streptopelia decaocto

YEAR-ROUND

Size: 12½" (32 cm)

Male: Head, neck, chest and belly are pale gray to a light tan. Slightly darker back, wings and tail. Black collar is bordered with white and extends around the nape of neck.

Female: same as male

Juvenile: similar to adult

Nest: platform; the female and male build; 2-3 broods per year

Eggs: 3-5; creamy white without markings

Incubation: 12-14 days; female and male incubate

Fledging: 12-14 days; female and male feed young

Migration: non-migrator

Food: seeds

Compare: Slightly larger and lighter in color than the Mourning Dove (pg. 149). Look for the black collar to help identify.

Stan's Notes: A non-native dove that is spreading into Colorado, having moved into Florida in the 1980s after being introduced to the Bahamas. Reaching the northern states beginning in the late 1990s, it is now expanding throughout North America. Predicted to spread throughout North America in the same way that it spread throughout Europe from the Middle East. Nearly identical to the Ringed Turtle-Dove, a common pet bird.

ROCK DOVE
Columba livia

YEAR-ROUND

Size: 13" (33 cm)

Male: No set color pattern. Gray to white, patches of iridescent greens and blues, usually with a light rump patch.

Female: same as male

Juvenile: same as adult

Nest: platform; female builds; 3-4 broods a year

Eggs: 1-2; white without markings

Incubation: 18-20 days; female and male incubate

Fledging: 25-26 days; female and male feed young

Migration: non-migrator

Food: seeds

Compare: Larger than light-brown-colored Mourning Dove (pg. 149).

Stan's Notes: Also known as Domestic Pigeon, it was introduced to North America from Europe by the early settlers. Most common around cities and barnyards, where it scratches for seeds. The wide color variation comes from years of selective breeding while in captivity. Parents feed young a regurgitated liquid called crop-milk the first few days of life. One of the few birds that can drink without tilting its head back. Nests under bridges, on buildings, balconies, barns and sheds. Once poisoned as a "nuisance city bird," many cities have Peregrine Falcons (not shown) that feed on Rock Doves, keeping their numbers in check.

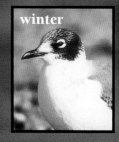
winter

breeding

FRANKLIN'S GULL
Larus pipixcan

SUMMER

Size: 14-15" (36-38 cm)

Male: Gray and white gull with a black head, and black extending partially down the neck. Black tip of wing separated by white band. Large white eye ring. Reddish bill. Winter has a partial black "hood" and black bill.

Female: same as male

Juvenile: brown back, black bill, lacks all-black head

Nest: floating platform; male and female build; 1 brood per year

Eggs: 2-4; greenish with brown markings

Incubation: 24-25 days; female and male incubate

Fledging: 31-33 days; female and male feed young

Migration: complete, to southern states, Mexico, and Central and South America

Food: insects, fish

Compare: Regularly occurring black-headed gull in the state. Look for it in open marshes, with a black "hood" and white wing tips.

Stan's Notes: Usually seen during spring and autumn migrations, when hundreds gather in prairie lakes. A three-year gull, the young don't obtain adult plumage until they reach 3 years. Juveniles are brown with partially black heads. The first- and second-year birds appear like winter adults, with gray and white plumage, partially black heads and black bills. Winters on the Pacific coast, all along Central and South America. Breeding range is from eastern South Dakota to western Minnesota and throughout Canada. Doesn't nest in Colorado.

soaring

COOPER'S HAWK
Accipiter cooperii

YEAR-ROUND
MIGRATION
SUMMER

Size: 14-20" (36-50 cm)

Male: A medium hawk with short wings and a long rounded tail with several black bands. Rusty breast and dark wing tips. Slate gray back. Bright yellow spot at base of gray bill (cere). Red eyes.

Female: similar to male, only slightly larger

Juvenile: brown back with brown streaks on breast, yellow eyes

Nest: platform; male and female build; 1 brood per year

Eggs: 2-4; greenish with brown markings

Incubation: 32-36 days; female and male incubate

Fledging: 28-32 days; male and female feed young

Migration: non-migrator to partial migrator, southern states and Mexico

Food: small birds, mammals

Compare: Nearly identical to the Sharp-shinned Hawk (pg. 219), only larger, darker gray and with a rounded-off tail.

Stan's Notes: A common hawk of the woodland. In flight, look for its large head, short wings and long tail. Short stubby wings help it maneuver between trees while pursuing small birds. Will come to feeders, hunting for unaware birds. Flies with long glides followed by a few quick flaps. Known to ambush prey, it will fly into heavy brush or even run on the ground in pursuit. Nestlings have gray eyes that become bright yellow at one year and later, dark red.

female pg. 159

male

GADWALL
Anas strepera

YEAR-ROUND
MIGRATION
SUMMER

Size: 20" (50 cm)

Male: A plump gray duck with a brown head and a distinctive black rump. White belly and chestnut-tinged wings. Bright white wing linings. Small white wing patch, seen when swimming. Gray bill.

Female: similar to female Mallard, a mottled brown with a pronounced color change from dark brown body to light brown neck and head, bright white wing linings, small white wing patch, gray bill with orange sides

Juvenile: similar to female

Nest: ground; lined with fine grass, and down feathers plucked from mother's breast; 1 brood per year

Eggs: 8-11; white without markings

Incubation: 24-27 days; female incubates

Fledging: 48-56 days; young feed themselves

Migration: complete, to southern states, Mexico, non-migrator in parts of Colorado

Food: aquatic insects

Compare: Male Gadwall is one of the few gray-colored ducks. Look for its distinctive black rump.

Stan's Notes: A duck of shallow marshes with lots of vegetation. Most commonly seen during spring and fall migrations. Returns to Colorado in May, with breeding in June. Nests on land within 300 feet (100 m) of water. Establishes pair bond during winter.

female pg. 161

male

BLUE GROUSE
Dendragapus obscurus

YEAR-ROUND

Size: 20" (50 cm)

Male: All-dark-gray chicken-like bird with bright yellow-to-orange patch of skin above eyes (comb). Shows white feathers surrounding an inflated yellow or purplish sac on the neck when displaying. Fans a gray-tipped, nearly black tail.

Female: mottled brown, gray belly, yellow patch of skin above eyes (comb)

Juvenile: similar to female

Nest: ground; female builds; 1 brood per year

Eggs: 6-12; pale white with brown markings

Incubation: 24-26 days; female incubates

Fledging: 7-10 days; female feeds young

Migration: non-migrator to partial migrator, will move around to find food

Food: insects, seeds, fruit, buds, conifer needles

Compare: The male Ring-necked Pheasant (pg. 173) is larger, with a long tail and bright colors.

Stan's Notes: The most common grouse of the Rockies, seen from the foothills to the timberline. Usually on the ground, but also seen in trees feeding upon newly opened leaf buds in the spring. Often switches from an insect diet in summer to conifer needles (Douglas-Fir) in winter. The male engages in elaborate courtship displays that include fanning the tail, inflating its brightly colored neck sac and singing (calling). Male mates with several females. Young leave nest within 24 hours, following the mother around to feed. Very tame and will freeze when threatened, making it easy to get a close look.

male

female pg. 169

NORTHERN HARRIER
Circus cyaneus

Size: 24" (60 cm)

Male: A slim, low-flying hawk. Silver gray with a large white rump patch and a white belly. Faint narrow bands across the tail. Tips of wings black.

Female: dark brown back, a brown-streaked breast and belly, large white rump patch, narrow black bands across tail, tips of wings black

Juvenile: similar to female, with an orange breast

Nest: platform; female and male build; 1 brood per year

Eggs: 4-8; bluish white without markings

Incubation: 31-32 days; female incubates

Fledging: 30-35 days; male and female feed young

Migration: partial to non-migrator, to southern states, Mexico and Central America

Food: mice, snakes

Compare: Slimmer than Red-tailed Hawk (pg. 165). Look for black bands on tail and a white rump patch.

Stan's Notes: One of the easiest hawks to identify. Harriers glide just above the ground, following the contours of the land while searching for prey. Wings are held just above the horizontal position, tilting back and forth in the wind, similar to Turkey Vultures. Was formerly called Marsh Hawk due to its habit of hunting over marshes. Nests on the ground. At all ages, the Northern Harrier has distinctive owl-like face disks.

CANADA GOOSE
Branta canadensis

YEAR-ROUND
MIGRATION
SUMMER
WINTER

Size: 25-43" (63-109 cm)

Male: Large gray goose with black neck and head, with a white chin or cheek strap.

Female: same as male

Juvenile: same as adult

Nest: platform; female builds; 1 brood per year

Eggs: 5-10; white without markings

Incubation: 25-30 days; female incubates

Fledging: 42-55 days; male and female teach young to feed

Migration: non-migrator to partial migrator, southern states

Food: aquatic plants, insects, seeds

Compare: Large goose that is rarely confused with any other bird.

Stan's Notes: Reintroduced into Colorado in the 1950s and 1960s after being eliminated early in the twentieth century. Adapting to our changed environment very well, they are now common year-round residents, breeding throughout Colorado. Adults will mate for many years, but only start to breed in the third year. Males often act as sentinels, standing on the edge of the group and bobbing their heads up and down, becoming very aggressive to anyone who approaches. Will hiss as if to display displeasure. Adults molt their primary flight feathers while raising young, rendering family groups flightless at the same time. Several subspecies vary geographically around the U.S. Generally they are darker in color in the western groups and paler in the eastern. Size decreases northward, with the smallest subspecies found on the Arctic tundra.

SANDHILL CRANE
Grus canadensis

MIGRATION
SUMMER

Size: 40-48" (102-120 cm); up to 7-foot wingspan

Male: Elegant gray bird with long legs and neck. Wings and body often stained rusty brown. Scarlet red cap. Red eyes.

Female: same as male

Juvenile: dull brown without red cap, yellow eyes

Nest: platform, on the ground; female and male build; 1 brood per year

Eggs: 2; olive with brown markings

Incubation: 28-32 days; female and male incubate

Fledging: 65 days; female and male feed young

Migration: complete, to southern states and Mexico

Food: insects, fruit, worms, plants, amphibians

Compare: Similar size as Great Blue Heron (pg. 239), but Crane has a shorter bill and a red patch on head. The Great Blue Heron flies with its neck held in an S shape, unlike the Crane's straight neck.

Stan's Notes: Among the tallest birds in the world and capable of flying at great heights. Usually seen in large undisturbed fields near water. Often heard before seen, they have a very distinctive rattling call. Plumage often appears rust brown because of staining from mud during preening. Characteristic flight with upstroke quicker than down. For their spectacular mating dance the performers face each other, bow and jump into the air while uttering a loud cackling sound and flapping wings. Often flips sticks and grass into the air during dance.

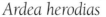

GREAT BLUE HERON
Ardea herodias

Size: 42-52" (107-132 cm)

Male: Tall gray heron. Black eyebrows extend into several long plumes off the back of head. Long yellow bill. Feathers at base of neck drop down in a kind of necklace.

Female: same as male

Juvenile: same as adult, but more brown than gray, with a black crown and no plumes

Nest: platform; male and female build; 1 brood per year

Eggs: 3-5; blue green without markings

Incubation: 27-28 days; female and male incubate

Fledging: 56-60 days; male and female feed young

Migration: complete, to southern states, Mexico, and Central and South America, non-migrator in parts of Colorado

Food: small fish, frogs, insects, snakes

Compare: Similar size as the Sandhill Crane (pg. 237), but lacks the Crane's red crown. Crane flies with neck held straight, unlike the Heron's S-shaped neck.

Stan's Notes: One of the most common herons, often barking like a dog when startled. Seen stalking small fish in shallow water. Will strike at mice, squirrels and just about anything else it might come across. Flies holding neck in an S shape, with its long legs trailing straight out behind. The wings are held in cupped fashion during flight. Nests in colonies of up to 100 birds. Nests in treetops near or over open water.

male

female

BLACK-CHINNED HUMMINGBIRD
Archilochus alexandri

Size: 3¾" (9.5 cm)

Male: Tiny iridescent green bird with black throat patch (gorget) that reflects violet blue in sunlight. Black chin. White chest and belly.

Female: same as male, but lacking the throat patch and black chin, has white flanks

Juvenile: similar to female

Nest: cup; female builds; 1-2 broods per year

Eggs: 1-3; white without markings

Incubation: 13-16 days; female incubates

Fledging: 19-21 days; female feeds young

Migration: complete, to Central and South America

Food: nectar, insects, will come to nectar feeders

Compare: Slightly smaller than the male Broad-tailed Hummingbird (pg. 243), which has a rosy-red throat patch and lacks a black chin. The flanks of female Broad-tailed (pg. 243) are tan, not white, like female Black-chinned's.

Stan's Notes: One of the smallest birds in Colorado and one of several hummingbird species in the state, these are the only birds with the ability to fly backward. Doesn't sing. Will chatter or buzz to communicate. Wings create a humming noise, flapping near 80 times per second. Weighing 2 to 3 gm, it takes about five average-sized hummingbirds to equal the weight of one chickadee. Males return first at end of April. Male performs a spectacular pendulum-like flight over a perched female. After mating, female builds nest, using spider webs to glue nest materials together, and raises young without mate's help. More than one clutch a year not uncommon.

male

female

BROAD-TAILED HUMMINGBIRD
Selasphorus platycercus

MIGRATION
SUMMER

Size: 4" (10 cm)

Male: Tiny iridescent green bird with black throat patch (gorget) that reflects rosy red in sunlight. Wings and part of the back are green. White chest.

Female: same as male, but lacking the throat patch, much more green on back, tan flanks

Juvenile: similar to female

Nest: cup; female builds; 1-2 broods per year

Eggs: 1-3; white without markings

Incubation: 12-14 days; female incubates

Fledging: 20-22 days; female feeds young

Migration: complete, to Central and South America

Food: nectar, insects, will come to nectar feeders

Compare: Slightly larger than the male Black-chinned Hummingbird (pg. 241), which has violet blue throat patch and a black chin. Female Black-chinned (pg. 241) has white flanks, unlike the tan flanks of female Broad-tailed.

Stan's Notes: Hummingbirds are the only birds with the ability to fly backward. Doesn't sing. Will chatter or buzz to communicate. Wing beats produce a whistle, almost like a tiny ringing bell. Heart pumps an incredible 1,260 beats per minute. Weighing just 2 to 3 gm, it takes about five average-sized hummingbirds to equal the weight of one chickadee. Male performs a spectacular pendulum-like flight over the perched female. After mating, female builds nest and raises young without any help from her mate. Constructs a soft flexible nest that expands to accommodate the growing young.

243

male

female

VIOLET-GREEN SWALLOW
Tachycineta thalassina

MIGRATION
SUMMER

Size:	5¼" (13.5 cm)
Male:	Dull emerald green crown, nape and back. Violet blue wings and tail. White chest and belly. White cheeks with white extending above the eyes. Wings extend beyond the tail when perching.
Female:	same as male, only duller
Juvenile:	similar to adult of the same sex
Nest:	cavity; the female and male build; 1 brood per year
Eggs:	4-6; pale white with brown markings
Incubation:	13-14 days; female incubates
Fledging:	18-24 days; female and male feed young
Migration:	complete, to Central and South America
Food:	insects
Compare:	Similar size as the Cliff Swallow (pg. 93), which has a distinctive tan-to-rust pattern on the head. Barn Swallow (pg. 69) has a distinctive, deeply forked tail. Tree Swallow (pg. 59) is mostly a deep blue, lacking any emerald green of the Violet-green Swallow.

Stan's Notes: Most commonly seen in the western half of the state. A solitary nester in tree cavities, but rarely beneath cliff overhangs, unlike colony-nesting Cliff Swallows. Like Tree Swallows, can be attracted with nest boxes. Searches for miles for errant feathers to line its nest. Short tail with wing tips extending beyond the end of the tail when perching. Returns to Colorado in April and begins nesting in May. Young often leave the nest by June.

GREEN-TAILED TOWHEE
Pipilo chlorurus

MIGRATION
SUMMER

Size: 7¼" (18.5 cm)

Male: A unique yellowish green back, wings and tail. Dark gray chest and face. Bright white throat with black stripes. Rusty red crown.

Female: same as male

Juvenile: olive green with heavy streaking on breast and belly, lacks crown and throat markings of adult

Nest: cup; the female and male build; 1-2 broods per year

Eggs: 3-5; white with brown markings

Incubation: 12-14 days; female and male incubate

Fledging: 10-14 days; female and male feed young

Migration: complete, to Mexico and Central America

Food: insects, seeds, fruit

Compare: Spotted Towhee (pg. 9) is black with rusty sides, appearing nothing like Green-tailed Towhee. Green-tailed's unusual color, short wings, long tail and large bill make it an easy bird to identify.

Stan's Notes: A common bird of shrubby hillsides and sagebrush. Surveys show it to be the thirteenth most numerous bird species in Colorado. Like other towhees, the Green-tailed searches for insects and seeds by taking a little jump forward while kicking backward with both feet. Known to scurry away from trouble by jumping to ground without opening wings, and then run across the ground.

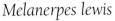

LEWIS'S WOODPECKER
Melanerpes lewis

YEAR-ROUND

Size: 10¾" (27.5 cm)

Male: Dull green head and back. Distinctive gray collar and breast. Deep red face and a light red belly.

Female: same as male

Juvenile: similar to adult, with a brown head, lacking the red face

Nest: cavity; the male and female build; 1 brood per year

Eggs: 4-8; white without markings

Incubation: 13-14 days; female and male incubate

Fledging: 28-34 days; female and male feed young

Migration: non-migrator to partial migrator, will move around to find food in winter

Food: insects, nuts, seeds, berries

Compare: Red-naped Sapsucker (pg. 35) has a black-and-white pattern on back and much more red on head. Male Williamson's Sapsucker (pg. 37) has a black back and large white wing patches, unlike the Lewis's dull green back and lack of wing patches.

Stan's Notes: Large and handsome woodpecker of western states. First collected and named in 1806 by Lewis and Clark in Idaho. During breeding season, it feeds exclusively on insects rather than grubs, like other woodpeckers. Prefers open pine forest and areas with recent forest fires. Excavates in dead or soft wood. Uses same cavity year after year. Tends to mate for long term. Doesn't migrate for winter, but moves to search for food such as pine nuts (seeds).

male

female pg. 157

NORTHERN SHOVELER
Anas clypeata

Size: 20" (50 cm)

Male: Medium-sized duck with iridescent green head, rusty sides and white breast. Has an extraordinarily large spoon-shaped bill that is almost always held pointed toward water.

Female: same spoon-shaped bill, brown and black all over and blue wing patch

Juvenile: same as female

Nest: ground; female builds; 1 brood per year

Eggs: 9-12; olive without markings

Incubation: 22-25 days; female incubates

Fledging: 30-60 days; female leads young to food

Migration: complete, southern states, Mexico, Central America, non-migrator in parts of Colorado

Food: aquatic insects, plants

Compare: Similar to the male Mallard (pg. 255), but Shoveler has a large, characteristic spoon-shaped bill.

Stan's Notes: One of several species of shoveler, so called because of the peculiarly shaped bill. The Northern Shoveler is the only species of these ducks in North America. Seen in small flocks of five to ten, swimming low in water with large bills always pointed toward the water, as if they're too heavy to lift. Feeds primarily by filtering tiny plants and insects from the water's surface with bill.

female pg. 275

male

COMMON MERGANSER
Mergus merganser

YEAR-ROUND
SUMMER
WINTER

Size: 27" (69 cm)

Male: Long, thin, duck-like bird with green head, a black back, and white sides, breast and neck. Has a long, pointed orange bill. Often appears to be black and white in poor light.

Female: same size and shape as the male, but with a rust red head, ragged "hair" on head, gray body with white chest and chin, and long, pointed orange bill

Juvenile: same as female

Nest: cavity; female lines old woodpecker cavity; 1 brood per year

Eggs: 9-11; ivory without markings

Incubation: 28-33 days; female incubates

Fledging: 70-80 days; female feeds young

Migration: complete, to southern states, Mexico and Central America

Food: fish, aquatic insects

Compare: Similar size as male Mallard (pg. 255), but male Common Merganser has a black back, bright white sides and a long pointed bill.

Stan's Notes: Mergansers are shallow water divers that feed on small fish in no more than 10 to 15 feet (3 to 4.5 m) of water. More commonly seen along rivers than lakes. The bill has a fine serrated-like edge to help catch slippery fish. Females often lay eggs in other merganser nests (egg dumping), resulting in broods of up to 15 young per mother. Male leaves the female as soon as she starts to incubate eggs. Orphans are accepted by other merganser mothers.

female pg. 171

male

MALLARD
Anas platyrhynchos

YEAR-ROUND MIGRATION

Size: 27-28" (69-71 cm)

Male: Large, bulbous green head, white necklace and rust brown or chestnut-colored chest. A combination of gray and white on sides. Yellow bill, legs and feet.

Female: all brown with orange and black bill, small blue and white wing mark (speculum)

Juvenile: same as female, but with yellow bill

Nest: ground; female builds; 1 brood per year

Eggs: 7-10; greenish to whitish, unmarked

Incubation: 26-30 days; female incubates

Fledging: 42-52 days; female leads young to food

Migration: partial migrator to non-migrator

Food: seeds, plants, aquatic insects, will come to ground feeders offering corn

Compare: The male Northern Shoveler (pg. 251) has a white chest with rust on sides and dark spoon-shaped bill.

Stan's Notes: A familiar duck of lakes and ponds. Will return to place of birth. The name "Mallard" comes from the Latin *masculus*, meaning "male," referring to the habit of males not taking part in raising ducklings. Both male and female have white tails and white underwings. Black central tail feathers of male curl upward.

male

female

RUFOUS HUMMINGBIRD
Selasphorus rufus

Size: 3¾" (9.5 cm)

Male: Tiny burnt-orange bird with a black throat patch (gorget) that reflects orange-red in sunlight. White chest. Green-to-tan flanks.

Female: same as male, but lacking the throat patch

Juvenile: similar to female

Nest: cup; female builds; 1-2 broods per year

Eggs: 1-3; white without markings

Incubation: 14-17 days; female incubates

Fledging: 21-26 days; female feeds young

Migration: complete, to Central and South America

Food: nectar, insects, will come to nectar feeders

Compare: The only hummingbird in the state that has this shade of orange (rufous) coloring.

Stan's Notes: One of the smallest birds in the state. A bold, hardy hummer, it is often seen well out of its normal range in the western U.S., showing up all along the East coast. Will visit hummingbird feeders in your yard. Doesn't sing, but will chatter or buzz to communicate. Weighing just 2 to 3 gm, it takes about five average-sized hummingbirds to equal the weight of a single chickadee. Heart pumps an incredible 1,260 beats per minute. Male performs a spectacular pendulum-like flight over the perched female. After mating, the female flies off to build a nest and raise young, without any help from her mate. Constructs a soft flexible nest that expands to accommodate the growing young. Doesn't nest in Colorado.

female pg. 301

male

ORCHARD ORIOLE
Icterus spurius

SUMMER

Size: 7-8" (18-20 cm)

Male: Dull orange bird with black head and black extending down the back. A black chin, tail and wings. Single white wing bars. A long, thin black bill with a small gray mark on lower mandible (jaw).

Female: olive green back with dull yellow belly, two white wing bars on dark gray wings

Juvenile: same as female, first-year male has a black bib

Nest: pendulous; female builds; 1 brood per year

Eggs: 3-5; pale blue to white, brown markings

Incubation: 11-12 days; female and male incubate

Fledging: 11-14 days; female and male feed young

Migration: complete, central Mexico, Central America and northern South America

Food: insects, fruit, comes to fruit/nectar feeders

Compare: Much darker orange than male Bullock's Oriole (pg. 261), with more black on the head and chest.

Stan's Notes: Prefers orchards or open woods, hence its common name. Eats insects until wild fruit starts to ripen. One of the last birds to arrive in spring and one of the first to leave each autumn, spending only about four to five months in Colorado. Usually nests alone, but sometimes in small colonies. Parents bring the young to jelly and orange half feeders shortly after fledging. Many people mistakenly think the orioles have left during summer but, in fact, the birds are concentrating on finding insects to feed their young.

female pg. 303

male

BULLOCK'S ORIOLE
Icterus bullockii

SUMMER

Size: 8" (20 cm)

Male: Bright orange and black bird. Black crown, eye line, nape, chin, wings and back with orange elsewhere. Bold white patch on the wings.

Female: dull yellow overall, pale white belly, white wing bars on gray-to-black wings

Juvenile: similar to female

Nest: pendulous; female and male build; 1 brood per year

Eggs: 4-6; pale white to gray, brown markings

Incubation: 12-14 days; female incubates

Fledging: 12-14 days; female and male feed young

Migration: complete, to Central and South America

Food: insects, berries, nectar, visits nectar feeders

Compare: The male Orchard Oriole (pg. 259) is much darker orange with more black on the head and chest.

Stan's Notes: So closely related to Baltimore Orioles of the eastern U.S., at one time both were considered a single species. Interbreeds with the Baltimore where ranges overlap. Most common in eastern Colorado, where cottonwood trees grow alongside rivers and other wetlands. Also found at edges of clearings, in city parks, on farms and along irrigation ditches. Hanging sock-like nest is constructed of plant fibers such as the inner bark of junipers and willows. Will incorporate yarn and thread into its nest if offered at the time of nest building.

female pg. 129

male

BLACK-HEADED GROSBEAK
Pheucticus melanocephalus

Size: 8" (20 cm)

Male: Stocky bird with burnt orange chest, neck and rump. Black head, tail and wings with irregular-shaped white wing patches. Large bill with upper bill darker than lower.

Female: appears like an overgrown sparrow, overall brown with lighter-colored chest and belly, bold white eyebrows, large two-toned bill

Juvenile: similar to adult of the same sex

Nest: cup; female builds; 1 brood per year

Eggs: 3-4; pale green or bluish, brown markings

Incubation: 11-13 days; female and male incubate

Fledging: 11-13 days; female and male feed young

Migration: complete, to Central and South America

Food: insects, seeds, fruit

Compare: The male Orchard Oriole (pg. 259) is only slightly smaller, but has a deeper orange-to-red breast. Not as much white on wings as the male Black-headed Grosbeak. Look for its large bicolored bill.

Stan's Notes: A cosmopolitan bird that nests in a wide variety of habitats, seeming to prefer the foothills in the western part of the state slightly more than other places. Breeds along two bands on the front range and western slopes from 5,000 to 8,000 feet (1,500 to 2,450 m). Both males and females sing, and aggressively defend their nests against intruders. Song is very similar to the American Robin's and Western Tanager's, making it difficult to tell them apart by song. Populations increasing in Colorado and across the U.S.

yellow male

female pg. 83

male

HOUSE FINCH
Carpodacus mexicanus

YEAR-ROUND

Size: 5" (13 cm)

Male: An orange red face, breast and rump, with a brown cap. Brown marking behind eyes. Brown wings streaked with white. A white belly with brown streaks.

Female: brown with heavily streaked white chest

Juvenile: similar to female

Nest: cup, sometimes in cavities; female builds; 2 broods per year

Eggs: 4-5; pale blue, lightly marked

Incubation: 12-14 days; female incubates

Fledging: 15-19 days; female and male feed young

Migration: non-migrator to partial migrator, will move around to find food

Food: seeds, fruit, leaf buds, will visit seed feeders

Compare: Male Cassin's Finch (pg. 267) is similar, but is a rosy red, unlike the orange red of male House Finch, and lacks a brown cap. Male Pine Grosbeak (pg. 271) is much larger. Look for the streaked chest and belly, and brown cap of male House Finch.

Stan's Notes: Very social bird. Visits feeders in small flocks. Likes nesting in hanging flower baskets. Incubating female fed by male. Loud, cheerful warbling song. Suffers a fatal eye disease that causes eyes to crust over. Birds east of the Rockies may be from eastern birds introduced to Long Island, New York, in the 1940s, which have since populated the entire eastern U.S. Rarely, some males are yellow (see inset) instead of red, probably due to poor diet.

male

female pg. 107

CASSIN'S FINCH
Carpodacus cassinii

YEAR-ROUND
WINTER

Size: 6½" (16 cm)

Male: Overall light wash of crimson red with an especially bright red crown. Distinct brown streaks on back and wings. White belly.

Female: overall brown to gray, fine black streaks on the back and wings, heavily streaked white chest and belly

Juvenile: similar to female

Nest: cup; female builds; 1-2 broods per year

Eggs: 3-5; white without markings

Incubation: 12-14 days; female incubates

Fledging: 14-18 days; female and male feed young

Migration: partial migrator to non-migrator, will move around to find food

Food: seeds, insects, fruits, berries, will visit seed feeders

Compare: Similar to the male House Finch (pg. 265), which has a brown cap, is heavily streaked on flanks and is orange red, unlike the male Cassin's rosy red. Much redder than any of the rosy-finches (pp. 3, 103 and 105).

Stan's Notes: Common high mountain finch of western Colorado, breeding in 8,000- to 11,000-foot (2,450 to 3,350 m) elevations starting in May or June. Usually forages for seeds on ground, but eats evergreen buds, and aspen and willow catkins. Colony nester, depending on the regional food source. The more food available, the larger the colony. Male sings a rapid warble, often imitating other birds such as jays, tanagers and grosbeaks. A cowbird host.

female pg. 297

male

RED CROSSBILL
Loxia curvirostra

YEAR-ROUND

Size: 6½" (16 cm)

Male: A dirty-red-to-orange sparrow-sized bird. Bright red crown and rump. Long, pointed, crossed bill. Dark brown wings and tail. Short tail.

Female: pale yellow chest, light-gray throat patch, a crossed bill, dark brown wings and tail

Juvenile: streaked with tinges of yellow, bill gradually crosses about two weeks after fledging

Nest: cup; female builds; 1 brood per year

Eggs: 3-4; bluish white with brown markings

Incubation: 14-18 days; female incubates

Fledging: 16-20 days; female and male feed young

Migration: non-migrator to irruptive, moves around in winter to find food

Food: seeds, leaf buds, comes to seed feeders

Compare: Smaller than male Pine Grosbeak (pg. 271) and lacks the wing bars. Look for the male Red Crossbill's unique bill.

Stan's Notes: The long crossed bill is adapted for extracting seeds from pine and spruce cones, its favorite food. Often dangles upside down like a parrot to reach cones. Also seen on the ground where it eats grit, which helps digest food. Plumage can be highly variable among individuals. Although a resident nester, migrating crossbills from farther north move to Colorado during winter, searching for food, swelling populations. This irruptive behavior makes them common during some winters and scarce in others.

male

female pg. 209

PINE GROSBEAK
Pinicola enucleator

YEAR-ROUND
WINTER

Size: 9" (22.5 cm)

Male: Plump rosy-red and gray winter finch with long dark tail. Dark wings have smattering of gray and two white wing bars. A short, stubby, pointed dark bill.

Female: mostly gray with dark wings and tail, head and rump tinged dull yellow

Juvenile: male has a touch of red on head and rump, female is similar to adult female

Nest: cup; female builds; 1 brood per year

Eggs: 4-5; bluish green without markings

Incubation: 13-15 days; female incubates

Fledging: 13-20 days; female and male feed young

Migration: non-migrator to irruptive, moves around to find food

Food: seeds, fruit, insects, will come to feeders

Compare: Much larger than the male House Finch (pg. 265). Male Red Crossbill (pg. 269) is smaller, with crossed bill and no wing bars.

Stan's Notes: Very tame and approachable bird. Often seen along roads or on the ground, eating tiny grains of sand and dirt to aid in digestion. A seed eater that favors conifer woods, rarely moving out of the conifer regions during summer. During the winter, it will move down from higher regions to the foothills in search of food. Often seen bathing in fluffy snow. Flies with a typical finch-like undulating pattern while calling a soft whistle. During breeding season, both male and female develop a pouch in the bottom of the mouth (buccal pouch) to transport seeds to young.

female pg. 153

male

REDHEAD
Aythya americana

YEAR-ROUND
MIGRATION
SUMMER

Size: 19" (48 cm)

Male: Rich red head and neck with a black breast and tail. Gray sides, and smoky gray wings and back. Tricolored bill has a light blue base with a white ring and black tip.

Female: plain, soft brown duck with gray-to-white wing linings, top of head rounded, gray bill with black tip

Juvenile: similar to female

Nest: cup; female builds; 1 brood per year

Eggs: 9-14; pale white without markings

Incubation: 24-28 days; female and male incubate

Fledging: 56-73 days; female shows the young what to eat

Migration: complete, to southern coastal states and Central America

Food: seeds, aquatic plants, insects

Compare: The male Northern Shoveler (pg. 251) has a green head and rusty sides, unlike the male Redhead's gray sides.

Stan's Notes: A duck of permanent large bodies of water. Forages along the shoreline, feeding on seeds, aquatic plants and insects. Usually builds nest directly on surface of water, using large mats of vegetation. Female lays up to 75 percent of its eggs in the nests of other Redheads and several other duck species. Nests primarily in the Prairie Pothole region of the northern Great Plains. The overall populations seem to be increasing at approximately 2 to 3 percent each year.

male pg. 253

female

COMMON MERGANSER
Mergus merganser

YEAR-ROUND
SUMMER
WINTER

Size: 27" (69 cm)

Female: A long, thin, duck-like bird with a rust red head and ragged "hair" on back of the head. Gray body with white chest and chin. Long, pointed orange bill.

Male: same size and shape as the female, but with a green head, black back, white sides and chest, and long, pointed orange bill

Juvenile: same as female

Nest: cavity; female lines old woodpecker cavity; 1 brood per year

Eggs: 9-11; ivory without markings

Incubation: 28-33 days; female incubates

Fledging: 70-80 days; female feeds young

Migration: complete, to southern states, Mexico and Central America

Food: fish, aquatic insects

Compare: Hard to confuse with other birds. Look for ragged "hair" on back of a red head, a long, pointed orange bill, white chest and chin.

Stan's Notes: Mergansers are shallow water divers that feed on small fish in no more than 10 to 15 feet (3 to 4.5 m) of water. More commonly seen along rivers than lakes. The bill has a fine serrated-like edge to help catch slippery fish. Females often lay eggs in other merganser nests (egg dumping), resulting in broods of up to 15 young per mother. The male leaves the female as soon as she starts to incubate eggs. Young that lose their mothers will be accepted by other merganser mothers with young.

winter

juvenile

breeding

RING-BILLED GULL
Larus delawarensis

YEAR-ROUND
MIGRATION

Size: 19" (48 cm)

Male: A white bird with gray wings, black wing tips spotted with white, and a white tail, as seen in flight. Yellow bill with a black ring near tip. Yellowish legs and feet. Winter or non-breeding adult has a speckled brown back of head and nape of neck.

Female: same as male

Juvenile: mostly gray version of adult, has dark band at end of tail

Nest: ground; the female and male build; 1 brood per year

Eggs: 2-4; off-white with brown markings

Incubation: 20-21 days; female and male incubate

Fledging: 20-40 days; female and male feed young

Migration: complete, to southern states and Mexico

Food: insects, fish, scavenges

Compare: Smaller than the California Gull (pg. 279), which has a larger bill with a red and black mark near the tip, and dark eyes, compared with the Ring-billed's light-colored eyes.

Stan's Notes: A common gull of garbage dumps and parking lots. It is expanding its range and remains farther north longer during the winter due to successful scavenging in cities. A three-year gull, acquiring a new and different plumage in each of the first three autumns. Attains the ring on bill after its first winter. Doesn't attain adult plumage until the third year.

winter

breeding

CALIFORNIA GULL
Larus californicus

YEAR-ROUND
MIGRATION
SUMMER

Size: 21" (53 cm)

Male: White bird with gray wings and black wing tips. A red and black mark on tip of yellow bill. Red ring around dark eyes. Winter or non-breeding adult has brown streaks on back of head and nape of neck.

Female: same as male

Juvenile: all brown for the first two years, similar to adult by third year

Nest: ground; the female and male build; 1 brood per year

Eggs: 2-5; pale brown or olive, brown markings

Incubation: 24-26 days; female and male incubate

Fledging: 40-45 days; female and male feed young

Migration: complete, to West coast and coastal Mexico

Food: insects, seeds, mammals

Compare: The only nesting gull in Colorado. Larger than the Ring-billed Gull (pg. 277), which lacks the dark eyes and red mark on bill.

Stan's Notes: Famed gull species that saved crops from an over-population of grasshoppers in 1848 and inspired gull monuments in Salt Lake City. A four-year gull, the first two years appearing nearly all brown. Third year is similar to the winter adult. Usually doesn't nest until the fourth year, when it obtains adult plumage. Common on reservoirs. Nests in large colonies of up to 1,000 nests at Riverside and Antero Reservoirs. The only gull species to nest in Colorado, with the first nest in the state confirmed in 1963. Named for its usual winter sites along the California coast.

SNOWY EGRET
Egretta thula

MIGRATION
SUMMER

Size: 24" (60 cm)

Male: All-white bird with black bill and legs, and bright yellow feet. Long feather plumes on the head, neck and back during breeding season.

Female: same as male

Juvenile: similar to adult, but backs of legs are yellow

Nest: platform; female and male build; 1 brood per year

Eggs: 3-5; light blue-green without markings

Incubation: 20-24 days; female and male incubate

Fledging: 28-30 days; female and male feed young

Migration: complete, to Gulf coast and Mexico

Food: aquatic insects, fish

Compare: The only all-white egret in Colorado. Look for the long black legs with yellow feet to help identify.

Stan's Notes: Common in wetlands and often seen with other egrets, colonies may include up to several hundred nests. Nests are low in shrubs 5 to 10 feet (1.5 to 3 m) tall or are on the ground, usually mixed among other egret and heron nests. Chicks hatch days apart (asynchronous), leading to starvation of last to hatch. Will actively "hunt" prey by moving around quickly, stirring up small fish and aquatic insects with its feet. In the breeding state, a yellow patch at base of the bill and yellow feet turn orange-red. Was hunted to near extinction in the late 1800s for its feathers.

blue morph

juvenile

white
morph

in flight

SNOW GOOSE
Chen caerulescens

WINTER

Size: 25-38" (63-96 cm)

Male: A mostly white goose with varying patches of black and brown. Black wing tips. Pink bill and legs. Some birds are grayish with a white head.

Female: same as male

Juvenile: overall dull gray with dark bill

Nest: ground; female builds; 1 brood per year

Eggs: 3-5; white without markings

Incubation: 23-25 days; female incubates

Fledging: 45-49 days; female and male teach young to feed

Migration: complete, to New Mexico and California, southern states and Mexico

Food: aquatic insects and plants

Compare: Smaller than the Canada Goose (pg. 235), lacking a black neck and white chin strap. Much smaller than American White Pelican (pg. 285), sharing the all-white body and black wing tips, lacking the enormous bill.

Stan's Notes: The more common white morph is pure white with black wing tips. Gray morph is often called blue, with white head, gray chest and back, pink bill and legs. Has a thick serrated bill for pulling up plants. Breeds in large colonies on northern Canada's tundra. Females don't breed until they are 2 to 3 years old. Older females produce more eggs and are more successful than younger females. Thousands seen migrating. Arrive in February and March; leave in April. Arrive in late September; leave by mid-December.

chick-feeding
adult

AMERICAN WHITE PELICAN
Pelecanus erythrorhynchos

Size: 62" (158 cm); up to 9-foot wingspan

Male: A large white bird with black wing tips that extend partially down the trailing edge of wings. A white or pale yellow crown. Bright yellow bill, legs and feet. Breeding adult has a bright orange bill and legs. An adult that is feeding chicks (chick-feeding adult) has a gray-black crown.

Female: same as male

Juvenile: duller white with brownish head and neck

Nest: ground; a scraped-out depression, rimmed with dirt; 1 brood per year

Eggs: 1-3; white without markings

Incubation: 29-36 days; male and female incubate

Fledging: 60-70 days; female and male feed young

Migration: complete, to Central and South America

Food: fish

Compare: Snow Goose (pg. 283) is much smaller and lacks the Pelican's enormous bill.

Stan's Notes: Often seen in large groups on larger lakes. American White Pelicans feed by simultaneously dipping their bills into the water to scoop up fish. They don't dive into water to catch fish, like the coastal Brown Pelican (not shown). Bills and legs of breeding adults turn deep orange. Breeding adults also usually grow a flat fibrous plate in the middle of the upper mandible. The plate drops off after eggs have hatched. They fly in a large V, often gliding with long wings, then all flapping together.

female

male

WILSON'S WARBLER
Wilsonia pusilla

Size: 4¾" (12 cm)

Male: Dull yellow upper and bright yellow lower. Distinctive black cap. Large black eyes and small thin bill.

Female: same as male, but lacking the black cap

Juvenile: similar to female

Nest: cup; female builds; 1 brood per year

Eggs: 4-6; white with brown markings

Incubation: 10-13 days; female incubates

Fledging: 8-11 days; female and male feed young

Migration: complete, to coastal Texas, Central America and Mexico

Food: insects

Compare: Yellow Warbler (pg. 295) is brighter yellow with orange streaking on the male's chest. Male American Goldfinch (pg. 289) has a black forehead and black wings. Common Yellowthroat (pg. 291) has a very distinctive black mask.

Stan's Notes: A widespread warbler of high elevations that extend down the middle of the state from north to south. Found in 6,000- to 12,000-foot (1,850 to 3,650 m) elevations near water in willow and alder thickets. Its all-insect diet makes it one of the top insect-eating birds in Colorado. Frequently flicks tail and spreads wings when hopping among thick shrubs, looking for insects. Females often mate with males that have the best territories and that might already have mates (polygyny). Nests in higher elevations produce more young than the lower elevation or coastal nests.

male

winter male

female

AMERICAN GOLDFINCH
Carduelis tristis

YEAR-ROUND

Size: 5" (13 cm)

Male: A perky yellow bird with a black patch on forehead. Black tail with conspicuous white rump. Black wings with white wing bars. No marking on the chest. Dramatic change in color during winter, similar to female.

Female: dull olive yellow without a black forehead, with brown wings and white rump

Juvenile: same as female

Nest: cup; female builds; 1 brood per year

Eggs: 4-6; pale blue without markings

Incubation: 10-12 days; female incubates

Fledging: 11-17 days; female and male feed young

Migration: partial migrator, flocks of up to 20 move around North America

Food: seeds, insects, will come to seed feeders

Compare: Pine Siskin (pg. 81) has streaked chest and yellow wing bars. The female House Finch (pg. 83) has a heavily streaked white chest. Male Yellow Warbler (pg. 295) is all yellow with orange streaks on chest. Male Wilson's Warbler (pg. 287) lacks black wings.

Stan's Notes: Most often found in open fields, scrubby areas and in woodland. Often called Wild Canary. A feeder bird that enjoys Nyger Thistle. Late summer nesting, uses the silky down from wild thistle for nest. Appears roller-coaster-like in flight. Listen for it to twitter during flight. Almost always in small flocks. Moves only far enough south to find food.

COMMON YELLOWTHROAT
Geothlypis trichas

SUMMER

Size: 5" (13 cm)

Male: Olive brown bird with bright yellow throat and breast, a white belly and a distinctive black mask outlined in white. A long, thin, pointed black bill.

Female: same as male, only lacking black mask

Juvenile: same as female

Nest: cup; female builds; 2 broods per year

Eggs: 3-5; white with brown markings

Incubation: 11-12 days; female incubates

Fledging: 10-11 days; female and male feed young

Migration: complete, to southern states, Mexico and Central America

Food: insects

Compare: Found in a similar habitat as the American Goldfinch (pg. 289), but lacks the male's black forehead and wings. The male Yellow Warbler (pg. 295) has fine orange streaks on chest and lacks the black mask. Yellow-rumped Warbler (pg. 193) has only spots of yellow. Male Wilson's Warbler (pg. 287) lacks the Yellowthroat's black mask.

Stan's Notes: A common warbler of open fields and marshes. Has a cheerful, well-known song, "witchity-witchity-witchity-witchity." The male performs a curious courtship display, bouncing in and out of tall grass while uttering an unusual song. The young remain dependent upon the parents longer than most warblers. A frequent cowbird host.

ORANGE-CROWNED WARBLER
Vermivora celata

Size: 5" (13 cm)

Male: An overall pale yellow bird with a dark line through eyes. Faint streaking on sides and chest. Small thin bill. Tawny orange crown, often invisible.

Female: same as male, but very slightly duller, often indistinguishable in the field

Juvenile: same as adults

Nest: cup; female builds; 1-2 broods per year

Eggs: 3-6; white with brown markings

Incubation: 12-14 days; female incubates

Fledging: 8-10 days; female and male feed young

Migration: complete, to coastal states, Central America and Mexico

Food: insects, fruit, nectar

Compare: Yellow Warbler (pg. 295) is brighter yellow with orange streaking on the male's chest. Wilson's Warbler (pg. 287) is also brighter yellow with a distinct black cap. Common Yellowthroat (pg. 291) has very distinctive black mask.

Stan's Notes: A widespread bird across the state during migration, breeding only in subalpine regions from 6,500 to 9,500 feet (2,000 to 2,900 m). Bulky, well-concealed nests are constructed on the ground with the rim of the nest at ground level. Known to feed at sapsucker taps or drink flower nectar. The orange crown tends to be hidden and is rarely seen in the field. A widespread breeder, from western Texas to Alaska and across Canada.

male

female

YELLOW WARBLER
Dendroica petechia

Size: 5" (13 cm)

Male: Yellow warbler with orange streaks on the chest and belly. Long, pointed dark bill.

Female: same as male, but lacking orange streaking

Juvenile: similar to female, only much duller

Nest: cup; female builds; 1 brood per year

Eggs: 4-5; white with brown markings

Incubation: 11-12 days; female incubates

Fledging: 10-12 days; female and male feed young

Migration: complete, to southern states, Mexico, and Central and South America

Food: insects

Compare: Look for orange streaking on chest of male. Orange-crowned Warbler (pg. 293) is paler yellow. Male American Goldfinch (pg. 289) has black wings and forehead. The female Yellow Warbler is similar to the female American Goldfinch (pg. 289), but lacks white wing bars. Similar to male Wilson's Warbler (pg. 287), which has a black cap, and lacks orange streaks on chest and belly.

Stan's Notes: Most widespread and second most common warbler in the state, seen in gardens and shrubby areas near water. Prolific insect eater, gleaning small caterpillars and other insects from tree leaves. Male is often seen higher up in trees than female. Female is less conspicuous. Starts to migrate in August. Returns in late April. Males arrive a week or two before the females to claim territories. Migrates at night in mixed flocks of warblers. Rests and feeds days.

295

female

male pg. 269

RED CROSSBILL
Loxia curvirostra

Size: 6½" (16 cm)

Female: A pale yellow-gray sparrow-sized bird with a pale yellow chest and light gray patch on the throat. Long, pointed, crossed bill. Dark brown wings and tail. Short tail.

Male: dirty-red-to-orange bird, bright red crown and rump, a crossed bill, dark brown wings and tail, short tail

Juvenile: streaked with tinges of yellow, bill gradually crosses about two weeks after fledging

Nest: cup; female builds; 1 brood per year

Eggs: 3-4; bluish white with brown markings

Incubation: 14-18 days; female incubates

Fledging: 16-20 days; female and male feed young

Migration: non-migrator to irruptive, moves around in winter to find food

Food: seeds, leaf buds, comes to seed feeders

Compare: Female Pine Grosbeak (pg. 209) is larger and has wing bars. Look for the female Red Crossbill's unique bill.

Stan's Notes: The long crossed bill is adapted for extracting seeds from pine and spruce cones, its favorite food. Often dangles upside down like a parrot to reach cones. Also seen on the ground where it eats grit, which helps digest food. Plumage can be highly variable among individuals. Although a resident nester, migrating crossbills from farther north move to Colorado during winter, searching for food, swelling populations. This irruptive behavior makes them common during some winters and scarce in others.

non-breeding
male

breeding male

female

WESTERN TANAGER
Piranga ludoviciana

MIGRATION
SUMMER

Size: 7¼" (18.5 cm)

Male: A canary yellow bird with a red head. Black back, tail, wings. One white and one yellow wing bar. Non-breeding lacks the red head.

Female: duller than male, lacking the red head

Juvenile: similar to female

Nest: cup; female builds; 1 brood per year

Eggs: 3-5; light blue with brown markings

Incubation: 11-13 days; female incubates

Fledging: 13-15 days; female and male feed young

Migration: complete, to Mexico and Central America

Food: insects, fruit

Compare: Larger male American Goldfinch (pg. 289) has a black forehead and lacks the breeding male Tanager's red head. The larger female Bullock's Oriole (pg. 303) lacks the female Tanager's single yellow wing bars.

Stan's Notes: The male is stunning in its breeding plumage. Most common in the western half of the state in elevations above 6,000 feet (1,850 m), from the foothills to the subalpine regions. Feeds mainly on insects such as bees, wasps, grasshoppers and cicadas. Feeds to a lesser degree on fruit. Male will feed the female as she incubates. Female builds cup nest in a horizontal fork of a conifer tree, well away from the main trunk, from 20 to 40 feet (6 to 12 m) above ground. The farthest nesting tanager species, reaching far up into Canada's Northwest Territories. Early fall migrant, often seen migrating in late July, with non-breeding males lacking red-colored heads. Can be seen in just about any habitat during migration.

male pg. 259

female

ORCHARD ORIOLE
Icterus spurius

Size: 7-8" (18-20 cm)

Female: An olive green bird with a dull yellow belly. Two white wing bars on dark gray wings. Long, thin black bill with a small gray mark on lower mandible (jaw).

Male: dull orange with a black head, chin, upper back, wings and tail, single white wing bars

Juvenile: same as female, first-year male has a black bib

Nest: pendulous; female builds; 1 brood per year

Eggs: 3-5; pale blue to white, brown markings

Incubation: 11-12 days; female and male incubate

Fledging: 11-14 days; female and male feed young

Migration: complete, central Mexico, Central America and northern South America

Food: insects, fruit, comes to fruit/nectar feeders

Compare: Female Bullock's Oriole (pg. 303) is more yellow with less distinct white wing bars.

Stan's Notes: Prefers orchards or open woods, hence its common name. Eats insects until wild fruit starts to ripen. One of the last birds to arrive in spring and one of the first to leave each autumn, spending only about four to five months in Colorado. Usually nests alone, but sometimes in small colonies. Parents bring the young to jelly and orange half feeders shortly after fledging. Many people mistakenly think the orioles have left during summer but, in fact, the birds are concentrating on finding insects to feed their young.

301

male pg. 261

female

BULLOCK'S ORIOLE
Icterus bullockii

SUMMER

Size: 8" (20 cm)

Female: Dull yellow head and chest. Gray-to-black wings with white wing bars. A pale white belly. Gray back, as seen in flight.

Male: bright orange and black, bold white patch on wings

Juvenile: similar to female

Nest: pendulous; female and male build; 1 brood per year

Eggs: 4-6; pale white to gray, brown markings

Incubation: 12-14 days; female incubates

Fledging: 12-14 days; female and male feed young

Migration: complete, to Central and South America

Food: insects, berries, nectar, visits nectar feeders

Compare: Female Orchard Oriole (pg. 301) is more green than yellow with more distinct white wing bars. Smaller female Western Tanager (pg. 299) has a black back, compared with the female Bullock's gray back.

Stan's Notes: So closely related to Baltimore Orioles of the eastern U.S., at one time both were considered a single species. Interbreeds with the Baltimore where ranges overlap. Most common in eastern Colorado, where cottonwood trees grow alongside rivers and other wetlands. Also found at edges of clearings, in city parks, on farms and along irrigation ditches. Hanging sock-like nest is constructed of plant fibers such as the inner bark of junipers and willows. Will incorporate yarn and thread into its nest if offered at the time of nest building.

male

female

EVENING GROSBEAK
Coccothraustes vespertinus

Size: 8" (20 cm)

Male: A striking bird with a stocky body, a large ivory-to-greenish bill and bright yellow eyebrows. Dirty-yellow head, black-and-white wings and tail, and yellow rump and belly.

Female: similar to male, with softer colors, and gray head and throat

Juvenile: same as female, but with a brown bill

Nest: cup; female builds; 1 brood per year

Eggs: 3-4; blue with brown markings

Incubation: 12-14 days; female incubates

Fledging: 13-14 days; female and male feed young

Migration: non-migrator to irruptive, moves around to find food

Food: seeds, insects, fruit, comes to seed feeders

Compare: Larger than its close relative, the American Goldfinch (pg. 289). Look for the dark head with bright yellow eyebrows and the extra-large bill.

Stan's Notes: One of the largest finches. Characteristic undulating finch-like flight. An unusually large bill for cracking seeds, its main food source. Often seen on gravel roads eating gravel, from which it gets minerals, salts and grit to grind the seeds it eats. It is more obvious during winter because it moves in large flocks, searching for food, often coming to feeders. Sheds the outer layer of its bill in spring, exposing a blue green bill.

WESTERN KINGBIRD
Tyrannus verticalis

Size: 9" (22.5 cm)

Male: Bright yellow belly and yellow under wings. Gray head and chest, often with white chin. Wings and tail are dark gray to nearly black with white outer edges on tail.

Female: same as male

Juvenile: similar to adult, less yellow and more gray

Nest: cup; female and male build; 1 brood a year

Eggs: 3-4; white with brown markings

Incubation: 18-20 days; female incubates

Fledging: 16-18 days; female and male feed young

Migration: complete, to Central America

Food: insects, berries

Compare: The Eastern Kingbird (pg. 203) lacks any yellow of the Western Kingbird. Western Meadowlark (pg. 309) shares the Western Kingbird's yellow belly, but has a distinctive black V-shaped necklace.

Stan's Notes: A bird of open country, often seen sitting on top of the same shrub or fence post. Hunts by watching for insects, such as bees, grasshoppers and crickets, then flying out to catch them and returning to its perch. Parents often bring wounded insects back to the nest to have young chase, thus learning how to hunt. Returns in April, nest building in May. Often builds nest in the fork of a small single trunk tree. More common in eastern half of the state, where nearly every stand of trees around a homestead or farm is home to a pair of Western Kingbirds.

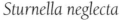

WESTERN MEADOWLARK
Sturnella neglecta

YEAR-ROUND

Size: 9" (22.5 cm)

Male: Heavy-bodied bird with a short tail. Brown back, lemon-yellow chest and a prominent black V-shaped necklace. White outer tail feathers.

Female: same as male

Juvenile: same as adult

Nest: cup, on the ground in dense cover; female builds; 1-2 broods per year

Eggs: 3-5; white with brown markings

Incubation: 13-15 days; female incubates

Fledging: 11-13 days; female and male feed young

Migration: non-migrator to partial migrator

Food: insects, seeds

Compare: Western Kingbird (pg. 307) shares a yellow belly, but lacks the Meadowlark's distinctive black V-shaped necklace.

Stan's Notes: Most common in open country of eastern Colorado. Named "Meadowlark" because it's a bird of meadows and sings like the larks of Europe. Best known for its wonderful song. Not a lark family member, it actually belongs to the blackbird family. Related to blackbirds such as grackles and orioles. Like other members of the blackbird family, the meadowlark catches prey by poking its long thin bill in places such as holes in the ground or tufts of grass, where insects are hiding. Opening its mouth to create some space, the bird extracts the bugs. Often seen perching on fence posts, it will quickly dive into tall grass if approached. Conspicuous white markings on each side of its very short and stubby tail.

HELPFUL RESOURCES:

Birder's Bug Book, The. Waldbauer, Gilbert. Cambridge: Harvard University Press, 1998.

Birder's Dictionary. Cox, Randall T. Helena, MT: Falcon Press Publishing, 1996.

Birder's Handbook, The. Ehrlich, Paul, David S. Dobkin and Darryl Wheye. New York: Simon and Schuster, 1988.

Birds Do It, Too: The Amazing Sex Life of Birds. Harrison, George and Kit Harrison. Minocqua, WI: Willow Creek Press, 1997.

Birds of Forest, Yard, and Thicket. Eastman, John. Mechanicsburg, PA: Stackpole Books, 1997.

Birds of North America. Kaufman, Kenn. New York: Houghton Mifflin, 2000.

Blackbirds of the Americas. Orians, Gordon H. Seattle: University of Washington Press, 1985.

Colorado Breeding Bird Atlas. Kingery, Hugh E. Denver: Colorado Bird Atlas Partnership and Colorado Division of Wildlife, 1998.

Cry of the Sandhill Crane, The. Grooms, Steve. Minocqua, WI: NorthWord Press, 1992.

Dictionary of American Bird Names, The. Choate, Ernest A. Boston: Harvard Common Press, 1985.

Everything You Never Learned About Birds. Rupp, Rebecca. Pownal, VT: Storey Publishing, 1997.

Field Guide to the Birds of North America: Third Edition. Washington, DC: National Geographic Society, 1999.

Field Guide to Warblers of North America, A. Dunn, Jon and Kimball Garrett. Boston: Houghton Mifflin, 1997.

Field Guide to Western Birds, A. Peterson, Roger Tory. Boston: Houghton Mifflin, 1998.

Folklore of Birds. Martin, Laura C. Old Saybrook, CT: Globe Pequot Press, 1996.

Guide to Bird Behavior, A: Vol I, II, III. Stokes, Donald and Lillian Stokes. Boston: Little, Brown and Company, 1989.

How Birds Migrate. Kerlinger, Paul. Mechanicsburg, PA: Stackpole Books, 1995.

Lives of Birds, The: Birds of the World and Their Behavior. Short, Lester L. Collingdale, PA: DIANE Publishing, 2000.

Lives of North American Birds. Kaufman, Kenn. Boston: Houghton Mifflin, 1996.

Living on the Wind. Weidensaul, Scott. New York: North Point Press, 2000.

National Audubon Society: North American Birdfeeder Handbook. Burton, Robert. New York: Dorling Kindersley Publishing, 1995.

National Audubon Society: The Sibley Guide to Birds. Sibley, David Allen. New York: Alfred A. Knopf, 2000.

Photographic Guide to North American Raptors, A. Wheeler, Brian K. and William S. Clark. New York: Academic Press, 1999.

Secret Lives of Birds, The. Gingras, Pierre. Toronto: Key Porter Books, 1997.

Secrets of the Nest. Dunning, Joan. Boston: Houghton Mifflin, 1994.

Sparrows and Buntings: A Guide to the Sparrows and Buntings of North America and the World. Byers, Clive, Jon Curson and Urban Olsson. New York: Houghton Mifflin, 1995.

Stokes Bluebird Book: The Complete Guide to Attracting Bluebirds. Stokes, Donald and Lillian Stokes. Boston: Little, Brown and Company, 1991.

Stokes Field Guide to Birds: Western Region. Stokes, Donald and Lillian Stokes. Boston: Little, Brown and Company, 1996.

Stokes Purple Martin Book. Stokes, Donald and Lillian Stokes. Boston: Little, Brown and Company, 1997.

For reporting unusual bird sightings or to hear a recording of where birds have been seen, contact:

Colorado Statewide	Western Colorado
303-424-2144	970-255-6193

WEB PAGES:

The Internet has become a valuable place to learn about birds. The following are a few web sites that will assist you in your pursuit of birds. You might find birding on the net a fun way to learn more about birds or to spend a long winter night.

SITE	ADDRESS
Colorado Field Ornithologists	www.cfo-link.org
American Birding Association	www.americanbirding.org
Cornell Lab of Ornithology	www.birds.cornell.edu
Author Stan Tekiela's home page	www.naturesmart.com

Use the boxes to check the birds you've seen.

ABOUT THE AUTHOR:

Stan Tekiela is a naturalist, author and wildlife photographer with a Bachelor of Science degree in Natural History from the University of Minnesota. He has been a professional naturalist for more than 20 years and is a member of the Minnesota Naturalist Association, Minnesota Ornithologist Union, Outdoor Writers Association of America and Canon Professional Services. Stan actively studies and photographs birds throughout the U.S. He received an Excellence in Interpretation award from the National Association for Interpretation, and a regional award for Commitment to Outdoor Education. A columnist and radio personality, his syndicated column appears in over 20 cities and he can be heard on a number of radio stations. Stan resides in Victoria, Minnesota, with wife Katherine and daughter Abigail. He can be contacted via his web page at www.naturesmart.com.

Stan authors several field guides for other states including guides for birds, birds of prey, reptiles and amphibians, wildflowers and trees.